C I T Y   O F   B I T S

The MIT Press, Cambridge, Massachusetts, London, England

Space, Place, and the Infobahn

CITY OF BITS

William J. Mitchell

First MIT Press paperback edition, 1996

© 1995 Massachusetts Institute of Technology

The book was set in Bembo and Meta by Wellington Graphics and was printed and bound in the Unites States of America.

Library of Congress Cataloging-in-Publication Data

Mitchell, William J.
  City of bits : space, place, and the infobahn / William J. Mitchell.
    p.   cm.
  Includes bibliographical references and index.
  ISBN 0-262-13309-1 (HB), 0-262-63176-8 (PB)
    1. Computer networks.   2. Information technology.   3. Virtual reality.
  I. Title.
  TK5105.5.M57   1995
  303.48'33—dc20   95-7212
                                                                      CIP

C O N T E N T S

CITY OF BITS

1

The infobahn goes in: telephone workers install fiber-optic cabling.

As the *fin-de-K* countdown cranked into the nineties, I became increasingly curious about the technicians I saw poking about in manholes. They were not sewer or gas workers; evidently they were up to something quite different. So I began to ask them what they were doing. "Pulling glass," was the usual reply.

They were stringing together some local, fiber-optic fragments of what was fast becoming a worldwide, broadband, digital telecom-munications network.[1] Just as Baron Haussmann had imposed a bold spider's web of broad, straight boulevards on the ancient tangle of Paris, and as nineteenth-century railroad workers had laid sleep-ers and steel to shrink the windy distances of the North American

frontier, these post-whatever construction crews were putting in place an infobahn — and thus reconfiguring space and time rela-tionships in ways that promised to change our lives forever.[2] Yet their revolutionary intervention was swift, silent, and (to most eyes) invisible.[3]

At about the same time, I discovered — as did many others — that I no longer had to go to work. Not that I suddenly became idle; it's just that the work now came to me. I did not have to set out every morning for the mine (as generations of my forebears had done), the fields, the factory, or the office; I simply carried a lightweight laptop computer that gave me access to the materials on which I was working, the tools that I required, and the necessary processing power. When I wanted to connect to the network, I could just plug it in to the nearest telephone socket or to the RJ–11 connections that were beginning to appear on airplane seats. Increasingly, I found that I did not even need to be near an outlet; my pocket-sized cellular telephone could do the job. Nor, in the age of the Walkman, did I have to go to the theater to be entertained. More and more of the instruments of human interaction, and of production and consumption, were being miniaturized, dematerialized, and cut loose from fixed locations.

How was the laptop on which I am writing these words (in an airport lounge) designed and built? Neither by an old-fashioned craftsman, lovingly contriving it like a Stradivarius violin, nor in some sprawling, smokestacked, Fordist factory. Its components and subassemblies were engineered and manufactured concurrently at locations scattered throughout the world — from Silicon Valley to Singapore. Computer-aided design (CAD) systems, computer-controlled processes, and industrial robots were used at every step. Component fabrication and product assembly operations were geographically separated, and component deliveries were carefully paced and orchestrated to avoid both shortages and unnecessary stockpiling. The various design, component manufacture, and product assembly tasks were performed not within a single industrial corporation, but by different members of an intricate international alliance. The finished product's software — which I chose and installed myself — is as crucial as the hardware. Now that this complex artifact is in my hands it is intensively used, but its useful life is short; soon it will be obsolete. When it can no longer connect me to the electronic information environment as effectively as some competing product (even though it still works perfectly well), I shall simply transfer my software and data and throw the superseded carcass away; the information ecosystem is a ferociously Darwinian place that produces endless mutations and quickly weeds out those no longer able to adapt and compete. Neither handicraft of the sort so passionately defended by Ruskin and Morris, nor durable, standardized, mass-produced, industrial object of the kind that fascinated the early modernists, my laptop is an emblematic product of the electronic information age.

The texts that follow reimagine architecture and urbanism in the new context suggested by these observations — that of the digital telecommunications revolution, the ongoing miniaturization of electronics, the commodification of bits, and the growing domination of software over materialized form. They adumbrate the emergent but still invisible cities of the twenty-first century. And they argue that the most crucial task before us is not one of putting in place the digital plumbing of broadband communications links and associated electronic appliances (which we will certainly get anyway), nor even of producing electronically deliverable "content," but rather one of imagining and creating digitally mediated environments for the kinds of lives that we will want to lead and the sorts of communities that we will want to have.

What does it matter? Why should we care about this new kind of architectural and urban design issue? It matters because the emerging civic structures and spatial arrangements of the digital era will profoundly affect our access to economic opportunities and public services, the character and content of public discourse, the forms of cultural activity, the enaction of power, and the experiences that give shape and texture to our daily routines. Massive and unstoppable changes are under way, but we are not passive subjects powerless to shape our fates. If we understand what is happening, and if we can conceive and explore alternative futures, we can find opportunities to intervene, sometimes to resist, to organize, to legislate, to plan, and to design.

2

"On the Internet, nobody knows you're a dog."

My name is wjm@mit.edu (though I have many aliases), and I am an electronic *flâneur*. I hang out on the network.[1]

The keyboard is my café. Each morning I turn to some nearby machine — my modest personal computer at home, a more powerful workstation in one of the offices or laboratories that I frequent, or a laptop in a hotel room — to log into electronic mail. I click on an icon to open an "inbox" filled with messages from round the world — replies to technical questions, queries for me to answer, drafts of papers, submissions of student work, appointments, travel and meeting arrangements, bits of business, greetings, reminders, chitchat, gossip, complaints, tips, jokes, flirtation. I type

E L E C T R O N I C   A G O R A S

replies immediately, then drop them into an "outbox," from which they are forwarded automatically to the appropriate destinations. (Note the scare quotes. "Box" is a very loose metaphor, and I will come back to that later.) If I have time before I finish gulping my coffee, I also check the wire services and a couple of specialized news services to which I subscribe, then glance at the latest weather report. This ritual is repeated whenever I have a spare moment during the day.

Traditionally, you needed to *go* someplace to do this sort of thing — to the agora, the forum, the piazza, the café, the bar, the pub, Main Street, the mall, the beach, the gym, the bathhouse, the college dining hall, the common room, the office, or the club —

and where you went pegged your peer group, your social position, and your role.[2] It also framed expectations about how you should represent yourself by your clothing, body language, speech, and behavior and about the interactions that were to take place. Each familiar species of public place had its actors, costumes, and scripts. But the worldwide computer network — the electronic agora — subverts, displaces, and radically redefines our notions of gathering place, community, and urban life. The Net has a fundamentally different physical structure, and it operates under quite different rules from those that organize the action in the public places of traditional cities. It will play as crucial a role in twenty-first-century urbanity as the centrally located, spatially bounded, architecturally celebrated agora did (according to Aristotle's *Politics*) in the life of the Greek polis and in prototypical urban diagrams like that so lucidly traced out by the Milesians on their Ionian rock.[3]

SPATIAL / ANTISPATIAL

Now, I just said that wjm@mit.edu was my name, but you might equally well (or equally inappositely) claim that it was my address. The categories are conflated due to the simultaneous redefinitions of space, personal identity, and subjectivity that are emerging as the network grows.

The Net negates geometry. While it does have a definite topology of computational nodes and radiating boulevards for bits, and while the locations of the nodes and links can be plotted on plans to produce surprisingly Haussmann-like diagrams, it is fundamentally and profoundly *antispatial*. It is nothing like the Piazza Navona or Copley Square. You cannot say where it is or describe its memorable shape and proportions or tell a stranger how to get there. But you can find things in it without knowing where they are. The Net is ambient — nowhere in particular but everywhere at once. You do not go *to* it; you log *in* from wherever you physically happen to be. In doing this you are not making a visit in the usual sense; you are executing an electronically mediated speech act that provides access — an "open sesame."

Your own address is not pinned to a place; it is simply an access code, with some associated storage space, to some computer located somewhere on the Net. It does not matter much what sort of computer it is or where you might find it. (I have never laid eyes on the machine that gives me access to the network. I suppose it is in some back room at MIT. There is no reason for me to seek it out.) To get on the network you establish physical connection to your host machine (through a digital link, by dialing in from any telephone via phone lines and a modem, or even via a cellular modem), provide the access code, and give a password. You can then ask the host to send you the accumulated contents of your inbox, and you can send it your outbox for distribution.[4] Other users of the network hook into their host machines in the same way. Thus, unlike telephone calls or fax transmissions, which link specific machines at identifiable locations (the telephone on your desk and the telephone on my desk, say), an exchange of electronic mail (e-mail) links people at *indeterminate* locations. If I send you an e-mail message, it will come tagged with my name/address, but you will not know whether I transmitted it from my office or typed it in at home while sipping a glass of wine or entered it into my laptop on a trans-Pacific flight and then sent it from a public telephone at Narita airport. And I need not know where you are — your current street address and zip code or your telephone number; I just direct my message to your network name/address, and I can be sure that it will eventually end up at whatever machine you choose to log in from.

If I wanted to be particularly careful about concealing my identity and location — perhaps because I intended to do something embarrassing like downloading pornography or illegal like grabbing pirated software copies — I could route my correspondence through an "anonymous remailer." This is a machine that functions like a numbered postbox or Swiss bank account; I can use it as an address that reveals nothing about me, and I can drop messages onto it for subsequent pickup.

So the Net eliminates a traditional dimension of civic legibility. In the standard sort of spatial city, *where* you are frequently tells *who* you are. (And who you are will often determine where you are allowed to be.) Geography is destiny; it constructs representations of crisp and often brutal clarity. You may come from the right side of the tracks or the wrong side, from Beverly Hills, Chinatown, East Los, or Watts, from the Loop, the North Side, or the South Side, from Beacon Hill, the North End, Cambridge, Somerville, or Roxbury — and everybody knows how to read this code. (If you are homeless, of course, you are nobody.) You may find yourself situated in gendered space or ungendered, domains of the powerful or margins of the powerless; there are financial districts for the pinstripe set, pretentious yuppie watering holes, places where you need a jacket and tie, golf clubs where you won't see any Jews or blacks, shopping malls, combat zones, student dives, teenage hangouts, gay bars, redneck bars, biker bars, skid rows, and death rows. But the Net's despatialization of interaction destroys the geocode's key. There is no such thing as a better address, and you cannot attempt to define yourself by being seen in the right places in the right company.[5]

CORPOREAL / INCORPOREAL

The incorporeal world of the Net has its own mechanisms for coding and class construction.

Some network acquaintances know me merely by the neutral identifier "wjm@mit.edu," for example, but most prefer to address me by one or another of my many more meaningful aliases. A few establish a direct linkage to a unique, known, embodied subject by listing me as "William J. Mitchell" in their personal directories of acquaintances, then select that alias as the recipient of their messages. My family, friends, and immediate staff, who send me messages very frequently, find it natural to use the abbreviated and more intimate alias "Bill." (It is not an ambiguous one in the bounded context of our acquaintance.) Proper names are not always necessary, though. Students, staff, and faculty at MIT often address their messages to "Dean," for instance, because that describes the role I play in their professional lives; if somebody were to replace me in that role, their messages could automatically, transparently, and immediately be redirected. My Finger file on the Net supposedly establishes who I am IRL (in real life), but it is itself just a set of potentially opaque or misleading descriptor values.[6]

Other correspondents address me implicitly rather than explicitly when they broadcast messages to groups defined by membership lists or by possession of specified characteristics — graduate students and instructors participating in particular seminars, researchers and scholars interested in certain topics, or just friends who sometimes like to do things together. (Membership of such groups separates the information-rich from the information-poor. Here, as elsewhere, class correlates with privilege.) Or they might find me by searching a database to find somebody matching a given profile.[7]

In this fashion, alias by alias, bit by bit, my disembodied electronic identity is constructed. But as Frege taught us in his famous analysis of "The Morning Star Is the Evening Star," it is not trivial, and perhaps not even true, to say that wjm@mit.edu is Dean@mit.edu or that either one is the embodied William J. Mitchell! When names float around without precise, unambiguous attachment to unique things, referential complexities abound.

It may even be that something with a definite electronic identity has no physical embodiment at all. Consider, for example, the Usenet Oracle.[8] You can e-mail questions to the Oracle, who resides in Indiana, and he will send you back answers. Whenever you submit a query, he will also send you another one and ask you to respond. He actually does nothing more than randomly match supplicants to respondents, and he is just a fairly simple piece of software. Yet he seems to have a personality and a characteristic sense of humor.

FOCUSED / FRAGMENTED

While I present myself to others on the Net through the aliases and descriptors I choose and the connections these aliases and descriptors establish, I also construct those others and they simultaneously construct me. (Different keystrokes for different folks.) But the process of mutual construction usually gives very little away. Because communication takes place without my bodily presence or the sound of my voice, others who "know" me quite well may not realize how I look or how I present myself in person, and thus may be unable to make the usual inferences from that.[9] (I am not inevitably subject to placement and displacement like Eliza Doolittle.) I can very easily conceal, leave carefully ambiguous, or falsely signal gender, race, age, body shape, and economic status. My representation on the Net is not an inevitability of biology, birth, and social circumstance, but a highly manipulable, completely disembodied intellectual fabrication; electronic cross-dressing is an easy and seductive game.[10] Conversely, I have found that it can be a jarring, dislocating experience actually to meet somebody I have long known through network interactions and for whom I have, by virtue of these interactions, presumptively devised a persona.[11] There are games of constructing electronic closets, and moments for coming out of them.[12]

On the Net I must present my password rather than my person whenever I want to identify myself — to show that it's really me. It follows that, if I can somehow obtain somebody else's password, I can, like an *Invasion of the Body Snatchers* alien pod, extinguish that poor soul from the scene and falsely assume his or her identity. (That person could do the same to wjm@mit.edu, of course.) Footsy with gender and social marking, and with the integrity of personal identity, need not stop here; I can create as many network identities as I want for myself, and others will have no way of knowing that these software-conjured zombies all belong to me. Try deconstructing *Invasion* not as campy allegory on cold-war commies but as a resistant glimpse into a world of unstable identities, ambiguously located intentions, and concealed control, and it looks very prescient.

My software surrogates can potentially do much more than provide origins and destinations for messages; when appropriately programmed, they can serve as my semiautonomous agents by tirelessly performing standard tasks that I have delegated to them and even by making simple decisions on my behalf.[13] (As the citizens of the polis relied upon their helots, so the users of the Net will increasingly depend upon their programmed agents.) It is a hacker's nobrainer, for example, to create a software receptionist — less politely known as a Bozo filter — that screens incoming electronic mail by checking the origin addresses, throwing away junk items, and sorting the rest in priority order. A slightly smarter agent might automatically contact other agents to reconcile diaries and arrange needed meetings at convenient times. (My agent will call your agent.) Another might sleeplessly monitor the stock markets for me, buying and selling according to some programmed strategy. Yet another might continually scan the wire service news to pick out items likely to interest me, and it might have the capacity to interrupt and alert me immediately when something really important shows up. And a more maliciously conceived one might be programmed to roam the digital highways and byways looking for trouble — for opportunities to corrupt the files of my enemies, to plunder valuable information, to eliminate rival agents, or to replicate itself endlessly and choke the system. Fritz Lang got it wrong: the robots in our future are not metallic Madonnas clanking around Metropolis, but soft cyborgs slinking silently through the Net. The neuromans of William Gibson are a lot closer to the mark.

While the Net disembodies human subjects, it can artificially embody these software go-betweens. It is a fairly straightforward matter of graphic interface design to represent an agent as an animated cartoon figure that appears at appropriate moments (like a well-trained waiter) to ask for instructions, reports back with a smile when it has successfully completed some mission, and appears with a frown when it has bad news. If its "emotions" seem appropriate, you will probably like it better and trust it more.[14] And if cartoon characters do not appeal, you might almost as easily have digital movies of actors playing cute receptionists, slick stockbrokers, dignified butlers, responsive librarians, cunning secret agents, or whatever personifications tickle your fancy.[15]

How do you know who or what stands behind the aliases and masks that present themselves?[16] Can you always tell whether you are dealing directly with real human beings or with their cleverly programmed agents? Was that politely phrased e-mail request for a meeting from wjm@mit.edu originated by the flesh-and-blood William J. Mitchell or was it generated autonomously by one of his made-to-order minions? (That, of course, was Turing's famous question. He thought that indistinguishability would demonstrate machine intelligence. But it might equally well follow from a human being playing dumb or engaging in discourses that do not require any smarts.) Does the logic of network existence entail radical schizophrenia — a shattering of the integral subject into an assemblage of aliases and agents? Could we hack immortality by storing our aliases and agents permanently on disk, to outlast our bodies? (William Gibson's cyberpunk antiheroes nonchalantly shuck their slow, obsolescent, high-maintenance meat machines as they port their psychic software to newer generations of hardware.)[17] Does resurrection reduce to restoration from backup?[18]

SYNCHRONOUS / ASYNCHRONOUS

A face-to-face human conversation — the sort for which dinner tables and traditional seminar and meeting rooms are designed — is a spatially coherent, corporeal, and strictly synchronous event. The participants are all present in the same place, everybody hears the words as they are spoken, and replies usually come immediately. The telephone and talk radio have allowed conversants to be dispersed spatially but have not altered this condition of synchrony. (Until the introduction of the answering machine, you had to be by the phone, at the right time, to take a call.)

But there is an alternative. Where necessary, as when Pheidippides was dispatched to run from Athens to Sparta and back, the ancient Greeks used messengers for asynchronous communication. The letter and the postal system, the fax machine, the humble home answering machine, and the fancy corporate voice mail system are all more up-to-date devices for asynchronous communication and so — more significantly in this context — are the network's e-mail and bulletin board systems.[19] In the asynchronous mode, words are *not* heard as they are spoken, but are repeated at some later point. Replies do not come immediately. The unity of the face-to-face conversation is fractured both spatially and temporally.

We usually find the laggardliness of the Postal Service's snail-mail, its enforcement of slug's-pace asynchrony, to be a nuisance. As much more efficient asynchronous communications systems have become commonplace, though, we have seen that strict synchrony is not always desirable; controlled asynchrony may have its advantages. We all know how inconvenient an unexpected demand for communication — a knock on the office door when one is deep in thought or a telephone call at the wrong time — can be. Business people and academics have gratefully discovered that it is usually much easier to communicate between Boston and Tokyo by fax than it is to find convenient times at both ends for telephone conversations. Answering machines and voice mail systems eliminate the frustration of telephone tag. You can attend to your e-mail whenever it is convenient to do so, not when you are unexpectedly and arbitrarily interrupted by a telephone ring. We are discovering that strictly synchronous communication is really just a limit case of asynchronous communication.

The tilt toward electronic asynchrony will have increasingly dramatic effects upon urban life and urban form. In the familiar, spatial, synchronous style of city, there is a time and a place for everything.[20] Gathering spots like restaurants and cafés are open, and people come together in them, for well-defined periods. Workers carry out their tasks during standard business hours, and there are predictable rush hours as they travel to and from their workplaces. Buses and trains have schedules, appointments and meetings are arranged for specific moments, theatrical performances, television programs, and university classes are slotted for particular times. Just as each city has its characteristic spatial organization, so it has its own daily, weekly, and seasonal rhythms — very different for New York, Rome, Delhi, and Tokyo. As there is prime real estate, so there is prime time. But now extrapolate to an entirely asynchronous city. Temporal rhythm turns to white noise. The distinction between live events and arbitrarily time-shifted replays becomes difficult or impossible to draw (as it often is now on the television news); anything can happen at any moment.[21]

When, for example, does an online forum take place, and where
do you show up for it? You cannot say. The discussion unfolds
over an indefinite period, among dispersed participants who log in
and out at arbitrary moments, through uncoordinated posting and
receipt of e-mail messages.

NARROWBAND / BROADBAND

The bandwidth-disadvantaged are the new have-nots. It's simple;
if you cannot get bits on and off in sufficient quantity, you cannot
directly benefit from the Net.

The consequences of this are brutally obvious. If the value of real
estate in the traditional urban fabric is determined by location,
location, location (as property pundits never tire of repeating), then
the value of a network connection is determined by bandwidth,
bandwidth, bandwidth. Accessibility is redefined; tapping directly
into a broadband data highway is like being on Main Street, but a
low baud-rate connection puts you out in the boonies, where the
flow of information reduces to a trickle, where you cannot make
so many connections, and where interactions are less intense. The
bondage of bandwidth is displacing the tyranny of distance, and a
new economy of land use and transportation is emerging — an
economy in which high-bandwidth connectivity is an increasingly
crucial variable.

Since the cost of a high-bandwidth cable connection grows with
distance, information hotspots often develop around high-capacity
data sources, much as oases grow up around wells. "Smart" office
buildings, for example, may have their own dish antennas for
satellite communications and fiber-optic links to the outside world,
and they provide internal broadband connections to these sources.
University campuses may connect their internal computer networks to long-distance telecommunications backbones, so creating

privileged, information-rich communities. Teleports, which concentrate powerful telecommunications equipment, may be built to serve industrial parks or financial districts.[22] And telecottages may play similar roles in rural areas.[23]

So some very contentious public policy issues start to pop up. The American telephone system was set up to provide "universal service" reaching not only to profitable markets for telecommunications services, but also to poor communities and to remote and sparsely populated areas where the costs of providing service are high and the customers are few. As part of the package, telephone companies became regulated monopolies, and unprofitable services were cross-subsidized by profitable ones. But will the fast lanes of the information superhighway — the switched, broadband, digital networks that will be required for the most advanced services — be deployed with the same lofty goal? Or will they serve only the affluent and powerful, while rural communities languish at the ends of information dirt tracks and economically marginalized neighborhoods get redlined for telecommunications investment?

Broadcast bandwidth is another matter — one of radiation epicenters and transmitter power rather than of network topology and cable capacity. There is only so much electromagnetic spectrum, so it is a definitively fixed resource in a given broadcast area. And there are only so many geosynchronous satellite "parking spaces" in the Clark Circle.[24] So powerful organizations will, no doubt, increasingly contend for shares of the bit radiation business in localities dense with receivers, and will seek like ancient despots to bring concentrations of population under their control.[25]

No network connection at all — zero bandwidth — makes you a digital hermit, an outcast from cyberspace. The Net creates new opportunities, but exclusion from it becomes a new form of marginalization.[26]

Since bandwidth costs money, most people still have to be content with very limited bandwidth access. And this cannot, of course, fully substitute for face-to-face (F2F) contact; only the most hopelessly nerded-out technogeeks could be persuaded to trade the joys of direct human interaction for solitary play with their laptops in darkened rooms. But what is the difference anyway? Just a few more bits.[27] (Hacker lore has it that burgeoning cyberspace romances progress through broadening bandwidth and multiplying modalities — from exchange of e-mail to phone and photo, then taking the big step of going F2F, then climbing into bed.) With improvements in telecommunications technology we can expect growing availability of higher bandwidth connections, which will make machine-mediated conversation and companionship seem better bargains.

Electronic interaction will become increasingly multimodal, as when videoconferencing combines sound and vision.[28] Robotic effectors combined with audio and video sensors will provide telepresence. Intelligent exoskeletal devices (data gloves, data suits, robotic prostheses, intelligent second skins, and the like) will both sense gestures and serve as touch output devices by exerting controlled forces and pressures; you will be able to initiate a business conversation by shaking hands at a distance or say goodnight to a child by transmitting a kiss across continents.[29] Exercise machines increasingly incorporate computer-controlled motion and force feedback and will eventually become reactive robotic sports partners (at any level of strength and skill you may choose). Today's rudimentary, narrowband video games will evolve into physically engaging telesports: remote arm wrestling, teleping-pong, virtual skiing and rock climbing.[30] Network pimps will offer ways to do something sordid (but safe) with lubriciously programmed telehookers.[31] (This is an obvious extrapolation of the telephone's transformation of the whorehouse into the call-girl operation.) Telemolesters will lurk. Telethugs will reach out and punch someone.

With higher bandwidths, ever-greater processing power, and more sophisticated input/output devices designed to take advantage of these capabilities, the boundary that has traditionally been drawn by the edge of the computer screen will be eroded. Through head-mounted stereo displays (an old idea of Morton Heilig's, which was first implemented by Ivan Sutherland in the 1960s and is now finally being popularized) or through holographic television (it's coming), you will be able to *immerse* yourself in simulated environments instead of just looking at them through a small rectangular window.[32] This is a crucial difference: you become an *inhabitant,* a *participant,* not merely a spectator.

The distinction between voyeurism and engagement that arises here can be a particularly critical one in contexts that traditionally have demanded presence. Paul Virilio has reminded us that seventeenth-century theologians debated whether a Mass seen by means of a telescope was valid.[33] They reasonably concluded that it was not, and still today, video participation in a Mass is reserved for the old, the infirm, and the disabled. But what about immersive, multisensory, telepresence at Mass? In a virtual church?

Once we have both a "real" three-dimensional world and computer-constructed "virtual" ones, the distinctions between these worlds can get fuzzed or lost. Ivan Sutherland's original head-mounted stereo display used prisms to insert simulated three-dimensional objects into real scenes. And through video projection of computer displays onto real desktops, or (as in some advanced military aircraft) through superimposition of computed stereo displays onto actual scenes, the proscenium dividing the "real" world from the "virtual" can be made to disappear. You can find yourself on stage with the actors, trying to distinguish the scenery from the walls.

CONTIGUOUS / CONNECTED

Spatial cities, of course, are not only condensations of activity to maximize accessibility and promote face-to-face interaction, but are also elaborate structures for organizing and controlling access. They are subdivided into districts, neighborhoods, and turfs, legally partitioned by property lines and jurisdictional boundaries, and segmented into nested enclosures by fences and walls. For the inhabitants, crossing a threshold and entering a defined place — as an owner, guest, visitor, tourist, trespasser, intruder, or invader — is a symbolically, socially, and legally freighted act. There is always a big difference between being a local and being an alien, being on your own turf and being on somebody else's, enjoying your privacy and appearing in public, feeling at home and knowing that you are out of place. So it is on the Net, as well, but the game gets some new rules: structures of access and exclusion are reconstrued in entirely nonarchitectural terms (if we continue to define architecture as materially constructed form), and you enter and exit places not by physical travel, but by simply establishing and breaking logical linkages.

Places in the cyberspace[34] of the Net are software constructions. Each piece of software running anywhere — on any machine or collection of machines in the Net — creates environments for interaction, virtual realms that you can potentially enter. The text window provided by a word processor is one such place. So is the "drawing surface" or "three-dimensional modeling space" within which you produce and view graphic constructions on a CAD system. So are the "desktops" and "file folders" provided by operating systems, the "cards" of Hypercard, and the "mailboxes" and "bulletin boards" of e-mail systems. Like architectural and urban places, these have characteristic appearances, and the interactions that unfold within them are controlled (often very rigidly) by local rules. A software "there" can be a one-dimensional place in a screen-displayed text; a two-dimensional place to put things on a "desktop" surface; a three-dimensional virtual room, storehouse, library, gallery, museum, or landscape; or even an n-dimensional place in an abstract data structure.

Some virtual places, like hermits' huts, can be occupied by only one person at a time. But others are designed to serve as shared-access, multiuser locations for joint activities — electronic calendars that can be updated by several staff members, CAD files that can be accessed simultaneously by several participants in a design session, or virtual chat and conference rooms. Sharing a virtual place is not quite the same thing, of course, as sharing a physical place like a room, a bed, or an umbrella in the rain. Bodies need not be in close proximity, and they need not be enclosed by the same architectural or natural boundaries. The crucial thing is simultaneous electronic access to the same *information*. At their simplest, shared places are created by displaying the same scrolling text on multiple personal computer screens. In more sophisticated places, inhabitants share the same two-dimensional graphic display or even the same immersive, multisensory virtual reality.

Shared "rooms" on the Net often announce themselves by descriptive or allusive names (like the signs on bars and other hangouts) — The Flirt's Nook, Gay and Lesbian, Red Dragon Inn, Romance Connection, Starfleet Academy, Teen Chat, Thirtysomething, Born-Again Onliners, Pet Chat, and so on. You can cruise them by scanning menus, and look in when they catch your interest, as you might bar hop down a street. The point (as in more traditional meeting places) is not just to be there, but to present yourself and to interact with others. Within these places, the participants must somehow greet and introduce themselves to one another, have some way of signaling that they want the floor, and follow some agreed convention for taking and relinquishing it. It can all be done simply by typing text or (if the available technology permits) by activating computer-animated body doubles.

Many of the places in cyberspace are public, like streets and squares; access to them is uncontrolled. Others are private, like mailboxes and houses, and you can enter only if you have the key or can demonstrate that you belong. (To get into my private electronic mailbox at MIT, for example, I have to identify myself and present a correct password to a gatekeeper agent named Kerberos.) And sometimes, as with movie theaters and hotel rooms, you have to pay to get in. But software walls — once erected — can be breached, locks can be broken, privacy can be violated, and turf can be trespassed upon, so cyberspace already has its outlaw hackers and phreaks and posses of lawmen chasing them, its viruses and Trojan horses, and its burgeoning mythology of transgression and retribution — those colorful tales of Acid Phreak and Phiber Optic, Clifford Stoll (the electronic sleuth) and Officer Phrackr Trackr, bumbling Keyboard Kops, the Pakistani Brain, the fabled Bulgarian virus factories, and the great virus-induced Internet Crash.[35]

You get from place to place in cyberspace by following logical links rather than physical paths. Sometimes, as for example in the graphical user interface provided by the Macintosh operating system, the places are nested to form a strict hierarchy: you go down a level in the hierarchy by clicking on a folder icon to open a "window" into a place, and you get back up a level by clicking on a corner of a window to close it — just as Dorothy clicked her heels to get back to Kansas. Alternatively, as in many hypermedia systems and adventure video games, the circulation system may be more freeform: each place provides clickable entry points to an arbitrary number of other places, and you can wander at will through the resulting labyrinth. (The symbols indicating these entry points may look like gateways or doors, but this is not essential.) To explore the whole, vast territory of the Net, you can use navigation programs like Gopher and Mosaic; these allow you to poke around in other people's computers at will, following the logical "paths" that relate machines, directories, and files.[36]

Click, click through cyberspace; this is the new architectural promenade.

BIT CITY

The network is the urban site before us, an invitation to design and construct the City of Bits (capital of the twenty-first century), just as, so long ago, a narrow peninsula beside the Maeander became the place for Miletos. But this new settlement will turn classical categories inside out and will reconstruct the discourse in which architects have engaged from classical times until now.

This will be a city unrooted to any definite spot on the surface of the earth, shaped by connectivity and bandwidth constraints rather than by accessibility and land values, largely asynchronous in its operation, and inhabited by disembodied and fragmented subjects who exist as collections of aliases and agents. Its places will be constructed virtually by software instead of physically from stones and timbers, and they will be connected by logical linkages rather than by doors, passageways, and streets.

How shall we shape it? Who shall be our Hippodamos?

3

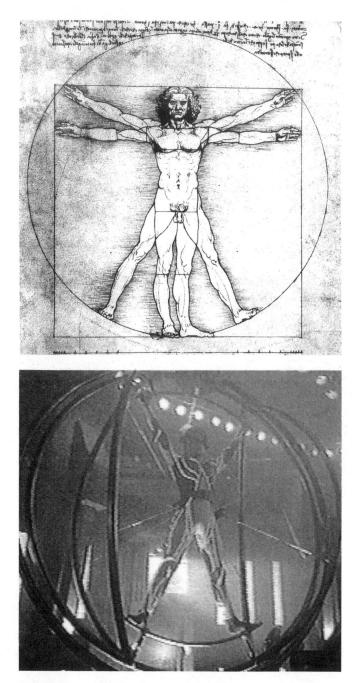

Bodies in space: Virtruvian Man and Lawnmower Man.

The sci-fi thriller *The Lawnmower Man* climaxes with a scene in which the fleshy body of the protagonist, Jobe Smith, is spread-eagled like Leonardo's *Vitruvian Man* in a whirling sphere, while his electronic avatar courses through the network. The camera cuts back and forth between the two conditions. As an ideally proportioned body inscribed in a circle evokes the humanist subject for which Renaissance cities and the buildings of Alberti and Bramante were made, so the fragmented figure of Jobe neatly suggests the incipient role of cities in the digital, electronic era — to house and delight subjects who have become sites of intersection between physical space and cyberspace.

VITRUVIAN MAN / LAWNMOWER MAN

Look around. The old body release — Monkeys 2.0 — no longer delivers what's needed; the users have been getting upgrade kits.[1]

I gaze from my window at the Nike-shod cyborgs on Memorial Drive. Their meat feet slap the surface of the solid world; their Walkman-augmented ears suck in signals from the virtual. Part-human, part-electronic jogging Januses, they have it two ways at once. Their bouncing bodies span different domains of existence.

Stephen Hawking, cyborg, speaks. Speaks? Stricken limbs and the Voltrax allophone generator built into his wheelchair team up to produce electronically mediated utterances. Immobilized flesh remains mute; fingers almost imperceptibly shift a joystick to select words from a displayed menu, then software and silicon retrieve stored sounds, assemble them into paragraphs, and emit them from speakers. Not the traditionally constituted body, but a new sort of electrosomatic construction now becomes the site of practice and project.

August 1991. Yo-Yo Ma, hypercellist, plays on the stage at Tanglewood.[2] His wrist, bow, and cello are all wired with special sensors. A computer translates the signals from these sensors into synthetic sound that a large audience hears through multiple speakers. Performer, instrument, computer, and speaker system become one cybernetic organism. Where are his/its boundaries?

Without leaving my office at MIT, I teach a class in Singapore. Like the cruelly immobilized physicist and the venturesome musician, I extend the limited affordances of my fleshy sensors and effectors through some ingenious electronic jiggery-pokery; a window opens on my computer screen and a distant video camera temporarily becomes my eyes and ears. I can control it from where I sit, as I would a camera in my own hands. At the same time, the students can see and hear me. I display and use my body at a distance. In an almost unconscious gesture, I adjust my tie in the video monitor — then realize with a start that I am not seeing a mirror but a picture of the picture that my audience views on the other side of the world. I am telepresent.

We are all cyborgs now.[3] Architects and urban designers of the digital era must begin by retheorizing the body in space.[4]

NERVOUS SYSTEM / BODYNET

Imagine that your wristwatch communicates continuously with your pocket computer; the computer's electronic clock provides the time information, so the watch reduces to a simple, conveniently located display with no internal time-keeping mechanism or adjustment buttons to push. Similarly, by connecting to the computer, your camera can get the information that it needs to time-stamp and date-stamp images. One central electronic clock takes the place of the three that would otherwise be needed, and all three devices are kept perfectly synchronized. The computer itself might grab information from the NIST atomic clock radio broadcast so that it never needs to be set.

Now extend the idea. Anticipate the moment at which all your personal electronic devices — headphone audio player, cellular telephone, pager, dictaphone, camcorder, personal digital assistant (PDA), electronic stylus, radiomodem, calculator, Loran positioning system, smart spectacles, VCR remote, data glove, electronic jogging shoes that count your steps and flash warning signals at oncoming cars, medical monitoring system, pacemaker (if you are so unfortunate), and anything else that you might habitually wear or occasionally carry — can seamlessly be linked in a wireless bodynet that allows them to function as an integrated system and connects them to the worldwide digital network. You will be able to use your PDA to program your VCR, listen to pager messages through your Walkman, display coordinates from the Loran on your smart spectacles, download physiological data from an electronic exercise machine into your PDA, and transmit the output from your camcorder to remote locations via your wireless modem. As you jog in a strange city, you might record your route on your PDA, then have your Walkman give you directions back to your hotel. You get the idea.

By this point in the evolution of miniature electronic products, you will have acquired a collection of interchangeable, snap-in organs connected by exonerves.[5] Where these electronic organs interface to your sensory receptors and your muscles, there will be continuous bit-spits across the carbon/silicon gap. And where they bridge to the external digital world, your nervous system will plug into the worldwide digital net. You will have become a modular, re-configurable, infinitely extensible cyborg.

Expect that electronic organs, as they become ever smaller and more intimately connected to you, will lose their traditional hard plastic carapaces.[6] They will become more like items of clothing — soft wearables that conform to the contours of your body; you will have them fitted like shoes, gloves, contact lenses, or hearing aids. Circuits may be woven into cloth. Microdevices may even be implanted surgically; electronic pacemakers and cochlear implants are now commonplace, neuromuscular simulation systems seem a promising way to repair spinal cord damage, there is intensive research into the possibility of implanted silicon retinas for the blind, and it is certainly not hard to imagine electronic ear studs, nose rings, or tattoos.[7] Some chips are tiny enough to be injectable and have already been used for tagging and tracking wildlife and identifying pets.[8]

Once you break the bounds of your bag of skin in this way, you will also begin to blend into the architecture. In other words, some of your electronic organs may be built into your surroundings. There is no great difference, after all, between a laptop computer and a desktop model, between a wristwatch and a clock on the wall, or between a hearing aid fitted into your ear and a special public telephone for the hard-of-hearing in its little booth. It is just a matter of what the organ is physically attached to, and that is of little importance in a wireless world where every electronic device has some built-in computation and telecommunications capacity. So "inhabitation" will take on a new meaning — one that has less to do with parking your bones in architecturally defined space and more with connecting your nervous system to nearby electronic organs. Your room and your home will become part of you, and you will become part of them.

But you will not even have to own the electronic organs to which you connect, and they will not have to be close by. Consider plain old telephone service; you rent channels and access to remote devices as you require them. This principle will be extended as digital networks grow in density of connection points, bandwidth, and geographic coverage and as different types of electronic organs are connected into them. We will all become mighty morphing cyborgs capable of reconfiguring ourselves by the minute — of renting extended nervous tissue and organ capacity and of redeploying our extensions in space as our needs change and as our resources allow. Think of yourself on some evening in the not-so-distant future, when wearable, fitted, and implanted electronic organs connected by bodynets are as commonplace as cotton; your intimate infrastructure connects you seamlessly to a planetful of bits, and you have software in your underwear. It's eleven o'clock, Smarty Pants; do you know where your network extensions are tonight?

For cyborgs, then, the border between interiority and exteriority is destabilized. Distinctions between self and other are open to reconstruction. Difference becomes provisional.

And perhaps, as the boundaries of the body and the limits of the nervous system become less definite, metaphysicians will be tempted to reformulate the mind/body problem as the mind/network problem. Some may want to argue that the seat of the cyborg soul   the postmodern pineal gland   is no longer to be sought just on the wet side of the carbon/silicon divide.

Eyes / Television

In the historic haunts of unaugmented humankind, space and time were continuous; a window divided inside from outside, but the very same place was always there on the other side, and there was no time difference across the glass. In the world that we cyborgs inhabit, though, the electronic retinas of our video cameras produce shifts and fragments. Rooms and buildings now have new kinds of apertures; the scenes that we see through the glass are rescaled and distant, the place on the other side may change from moment to moment, and the action may be a replay.

Punch anticipated this in 1879: a cartoon showed the imagined "Edison's Telephonoscope (transmits light as well as sound)" opening up a video window above the bedroom mantelpiece of a comfortable Victorian villa. Paterfamilias and materfamilias in Wilton Place were seen teleconferencing with their children in antipodean Ceylon. The electric camera obscura was soon, in fact, a reality: in 1884 Paul Nipkow patented the Nipkow disk system for electromechanically converting pictures into electrical signals and then decoding them at a reception point; in 1926 John Logie Baird produced a television system that really worked, and from 1929 to 1937 the BBC used the Baird system to provide broadcast television service; in 1939 at the New York World's Fair RCA unveiled its electronic, CRT-based television system; in 1975 cable television operators begin to receive programming from communications satellites.[9] A century after the prescient *Punch* cartoon appeared, C-Span and CNN went on the air.

Late afternoon, Cambridge, England. I sit at the desk of a Xerox PARC researcher. Outside, through the grimy window to the street, I can glimpse the sun setting over stone spires. Simultaneously, through the electronic window before me, I see an empty office at Xerox PARC headquarters in Palo Alto, California. And, through the window of that distant office, that same sun is visible rising over the ochre Palo Alto hills. I am in the media space that has been constructed to weld two distant office buildings together by adding continuously open, two-way, electronic windows at both ends.[10]

Fancy hotel room, Riyadh. A one-way electronic window opens onto the CNN newsroom in Atlanta. An arrow on the bedside table points the prayerful to Mecca, but the satellite dish on the roof turns news junkies and insomniacs toward Georgia. An amplified muezzin, calling from somewhere outside, marks the moment for morning devotions; beyond the electronic window, the news anchor greets the top of the hour with a fast-paced rundown of the day's top stories. Right now, the same window is open in thousands and thousands of similar hotel rooms spread around the world. Ted Turner has succeeded in electronically organizing them all into a gigantic, inverted panopticon. But the antipanoptic center — the place that draws gazes from all the scattered cyborg cells — can be switched instantaneously; as we watch, it moves to London, then to Sydney, to Beijing, then back to Atlanta. And it can slide back in time as signals generated from video recordings (which have become visually indistinguishable from live camera output) are switched into the transmission.

House of Microsoft mogul Bill Gates, Seattle. The interior wall panels are not what they seem. They turn out to be huge, flat video screens. In repose they simulate the surfaces of standard architectural materials, but activated they become electronic windows opening onto anything at all. Architectural solids and voids become fluidly interchangeable, and the usual relationship of interior to exterior space is twisted into jaw-dropping paradox. That old *Punch* cartoon flashes again into my mind.

Kresge Auditorium, MIT. A conference is assembled in honor of artificial intelligence pioneer Marvin Minsky. On stage is a hole in space — a video window into a book-lined study in Sri Lanka (the former British colony of Ceylon). Without leaving his tropical home, Arthur C. Clarke steps into view, delivers the keynote, and fields questions from the audience. In 1993 this is still fairly unusual — a tour-de-force of jury-rigged electronics — but the business pages tell us, and the audience is abuzz with talk, of the feverish rush to wire American communities for two-way, interactive video. Soon we will be able casually to create holes in space wherever and whenever we want them.[11] Every place with a network connection will potentially have every other such place just outside the window.

Once, places were bounded by walls and horizons. Days were defined by sunrises and sunsets. But we video cyborgs see things differently. The Net has become a worldwide, time-zone-spanning optic nerve with electronic eyeballs at its endpoints.

Ears / Telephony

Café Peón Contreras, Mérida. A trio sings and plays as I drink Montejo beer. It's a familiar, traditional arrangement. The musicians and the audience are within easy sight and earshot of each other in a public place, and the music holds us all in a face-to-face, synchronized relationship for as long as the performance lasts.

Around the same time, Frank Sinatra's fading voice croaks duets with a clutch of mostly unlikely partners.[12] But his ol' blue eyes don't see them, and the audience doesn't assemble in his bodily presence. It's One More for My Baby and One More for the Information Superhighway. Sinatra remains concealed in a Capitol Records studio in Hollywood, while strangers on the Net, far more than just a glance away, telecroon in their tracks over distortion-free fiber-optic lines — Tony Bennett doing "New York, New York" from Manhattan, Liza Minelli from Brazil, Aretha Franklin from Detroit, and so on across the globe.[13] (The time delay, unlike the delay with a satellite link, is imperceptible.) Producer Phil Ramone digitally assembles these disembodied vocals, and I finally hear the result on my rental car stereo — along with thousands of other commuters tuned to the same station — as I sit in morning traffic on the Bay Bridge to Oakland. A *New York Times* critic harrumphs: "No matter how gratifying the results, however, can they be called duets? A duet implies spontaneous interaction and mutual responsiveness between two performers in each other's presence, a condition obviously not met by a recording of performers widely separated in time and space. To call the disk 'Duets' seems a misnomer."[14]

The Mérida trio performance takes *place* at a certain spot and has its particular evening hour. And I am *there* in the old-fashioned way: in person, unplugged. The problematic Sinatra duets, though, are constructed in cyberspace by cyborgs of a species that began to emerge on March 10, 1876, when Alexander Graham Bell, Professor of Vocal Physiology in the School of Oratory of Boston University, first successfully connected an electromechanical ear to an electromechanical voice box by an electric wire. And I can listen in *only* with the aid of my own artificial audio organs; if I tried to get within actual earshot of the performance, I would most certainly find that there's no there there. Not only have the configurations of our bodies changed — with their now endlessly multiplied, displaced, and time-shifted speech and hearing organs — but also their relationships to the city's spaces and temporal rhythms.

Telephony did not replace face-to-face human contact; indeed, Bell's very first telephone message was "Mr. Watson — come here — I want to see you." Rather, it created a new form of contact; it extended and redefined the sphere of interaction and inhabitation. Now familiar, this acoustic hyperextension once seemed spooky; Avital Ronell reminds us that the circus showman Phineas T. Barnum "was loath to display the telephone, because he didn't wish to freak out his audience with this voiced partial limb, no doubt, whereas limbless figures were still held to be digestible."[15]

Barnum's suckers would have been even more stupefied by the Convolvotron — a clever, recently invented digital device that places electronically synthesized or recreated sounds in particular locations.[16] It can surround us with virtual cocktail parties of voices that seem to come from empty points in space.

But we're different now. We telephonic cyborgs are comfortably at home in a world of disembodied sounds — of speech displaced in space and time from its origins, of performances that do not require stages or places to assemble audiences, and of conversations without the confrontation of bodies. And we meet in places that cannot be found on city maps.

MUSCLES / ACTUATORS

Suddenly I feel the shock of a major earthquake, but it doesn't bother me a bit; I'm playing around on a hydraulically actuated, computer-controlled shaking table — a device that is more normally used to test structural prototypes for seismic safety — and I'm experiencing a simulation generated from seismograph data. Mechanical muscles move my body.

Luxor hotel-casino, Las Vegas. Along with other paying customers, I strap myself into an even more advanced kind of motion simulator.[17] A wide-angle screen before us presents a pilot's-eye view of a high-speed, twisting, turning, diving flight through a fantastic three-dimensional environment, and the accelerations of our seats are precisely synchronized with the projected images to produce the corresponding g-forces and jolts. It is a scary, stomach-churning roller coaster ride through a vast virtual landscape, but we never actually move more than a few feet, and from beginning to end we don't leave the same small, darkened room. The phenomenal motion is far greater than the actual motion; it's all in the cunning programming.

Anaheim Convention Center. I line up with the computer graphics geeks and off-duty demo-dollies to check out the Sega R360. Doug Trumbull's Luxor ride milks all of its thrills out of sliding motions along just two axes, but this one does 360-degree rotations. And I strap on a head-mounted display instead of watching a projection screen. The illusion of flying like Superman is complete. Killer vestibulars!

Physical movement and phenomenal motion can now be disconnected; we teleporting cyborgs have found loopholes in Newton's laws.

HANDS / TELEMANIPULATORS

An operating table; a surgeon's scalpel moves precisely across the surface of an eyeball to make a delicate incision. But the scalpel is teleoperated, and the surgeon is hundreds of miles away, grasping a force-feedback device and watching the output from a medical imaging system on a video monitor.

Actually, this scene is a simulation, and the scalpel is merely cutting into a grape. But by the early 1990s robotic surgery and telesurgery had been active research topics for some time, and there had been many such experiments. Tissue removal had been practiced on chicken breasts, brain surgery on watermelons.[18] And there had been some successful practical applications of robotic devices to surgical tasks requiring positional certainty and rapid performance: in March 1991, at Shaftesbury Hospital in London, the world's first active surgical robot was used to perform prostate surgery on a live patient,[19] and in November 1992 Robodoc — a specialized robotic arm — helped replace the arthritic hip of a sixty-four-year-old Sacramento man.[20] Specialized telemanipulators were becoming an increasingly important part of the cyborg organ repertoire.

There are endless reasons for robotically extending your reach. If you are a skilled surgeon, you might want to make your capabilities more widely available through use of remote manipulation techniques, or you might just want to stay well away from dangerous places like battlefields or the South Side of Chicago. If you are an astronomer, you might wish to use a telescope without actually having to go to some distant, isolated site. If you are a vulcanologist, you might not want to climb down into an active crater to take a look.[21] If you are a construction machinery operator, you might rather work from the comfort and safety of an air-conditioned site office than from a vertiginous, noisy, dusty cab.[22] If you are a cop or a bomb disposal specialist, you might very understandably want to get a dangerous job done without having to put your flesh on the line.[23] If you are a planetary geologist, you may simply have no way of getting your own body to the terrain that you want to explore.[24] And if you are in your right mind, you will not want to get too cozy with infectious samples in a medical laboratory or with a nuclear power plant or hazardous chemical plant in an emergency situation. Just equip yourself with the right sorts of video eyes and electromechanical hands.

Just as boxers with long arms stand less chance of getting belted in the jaw than opponents with shorter reaches, so cyborg soldiers equipped with teleoperated weapons can stay safely in the rear echelon and avoid the dangers of front-line combat. In the Gulf War, for the first time, teleoperated weapons actually played a significant battlefield role.[25] The sky was abuzz with Pioneer RPVs (remotely piloted vehicles) — teleoperated, pilotless planes that were used to track Iraqi forces, spot missile sites, search for mines, and survey bomb damage. The 82nd Airborne used Pointer RPVs to patrol base perimeters, and German mine sweepers deployed teleoperated patrol boats. In the future, the hand that holds the weapon may grow even longer: a 1987 *Military Review* article speculated, "In a physiological sense, when needed, soldiers may actually appear to be three miles tall and twenty miles wide . . . we might hope to create future warriors that we could send forward surrounded by protecting robots or remote control aircraft."[26] Goliath is being reinvented.

Conversely, if robotic devices are constructed at insect size, they can also be used to get closer than we otherwise could and thus to manipulate things that are too small to be grasped by the fingertips. Rodney Brooks contrived a cockroach-sized robot at MIT in 1988, then set to work on piezoelectric motor-powered ant robots about a millimeter across. These might, he suggested, be used to crawl into arteries and unclog them, reconnect severed neurons, or skate across eyeballs to perform retinal surgery.[27] Tiny telemanipulators and robots seem particularly well suited to laparoscopic surgery, in which instruments and cameras are inserted through very small incisions in the body while the surgeon watches a video monitor, perhaps from a remote location. Johannes Smits of Boston University, inventor of a micromotor device, has suggested that minute electromechanical bugs could also act as miniature spies: "Imagine what you could do with an ant if you could control it. You could make it walk into CIA headquarters."[28]

By using a microscope instead of an ordinary video camera and a micromanipulator in place of a human-scaled telerobot, you can go right down to the atomic scale and act in the world you find there. The UNC/UCLA nanomanipulator, for example, employs a head-mounted stereo display to view data from a scanning-tunneling microscope in real time and makes use of the microscope probe tip as a manipulator. A force-feedback arm provides the effect of running a nanoscaled hand across the displayed surfaces and pushing things around.[29] Ultra-Lilliputian nanorobots — which have at least been the subject of serious speculation — could submarine through veins and arteries and perform molecular-level surgery.[30]

All this is the outcome of an evolutionary process that began in the second half of the eighteenth century, when scientists began to play with the idea of accomplishing action at a distance by sending electricity through wires.[31] Early experiments produced sparks or moved pith balls. By the early nineteenth century there was much scientific speculation about the possibility of telegraphy — writing at a distance. By 1843 Samuel Morse had successfully constructed a long-distance telegraph line between Washington and Baltimore, and opened it with the Morse-coded message "What hath God wrought." By the 1890s William Crookes was imagining the "new and astonishing" possibility of wireless telegraphy, and as the twentieth century dawned Guglielmo Marconi transmitted a wireless signal across the Atlantic. (Marconi's first transatlantic message was one of modernist minimalism — a single pulse, just one bit of information.) Now, any device connected to the worldwide telecommunications network is potentially a site for action by anyone anywhere on that net. So virtual reality researcher Warren Robinett has extrapolated from the telegraph to bodily telepresence: "In a few years visual telepresence may be widely available, so that a person can move by virtual travel instantly to distant locations, just as it is now possible with the telephone for hearing only. If, at that time, most controllable devices are linked to the communications network, then it will be possible for a person to project by virtual travel to a distant location and initiate actions there through the actuators available at that site."[32]

Unlike Leonardo's Vitruvian Man, we telemanipulating cyborgs cannot be encircled by neat arcs swept through our outstretched limbs. Our grasp has no limits — upper or lower. We have no fixed scale.

BRAINS / ARTIFICIAL INTELLIGENCE

An anonymous street in Tokyo. As usual in this huge and confusing metropolis, I have absolutely no idea where I am. So my companion casually punches a button on the dashboard of his car, and the latest Japanese consumer electronics wonder beeps into action. It instantly grabs our coordinates from the global positioning satellite system, displays a detailed street map on a dashboard screen, and indicates our position and direction with an arrow.[33] As we navigate the intricate route from Shinjuku to Asakusa, the system continuously updates the display to reflect our current location — automatically rotating and recentering the map to keep the arrow just below the middle of the map and pointing straight ahead. The real city that surrounds us and the video city that guides us are held in perfect coincidence.

But this is just the beginning. A vehicle that knows where it is, and can pull information relevant to its location out of a database of geographically coded information, can do a lot more than display maps.[34] For example, it might look up interesting facts in online guidebooks and read you a commentary on the passing scene. With slightly more sophisticated programming, it could learn what you particularly cared about — the highlights of local history, perhaps, or census information, or the agricultural products of the area — and, like a knowledgeable and attentive companion, it could offer only observations likely to interest you. If you were driving a delivery truck, looking at real estate, canvassing for a political cause, or performing some other specialized task requiring information about passing buildings and their occupants, the system could supply it. For travelers it could deal with some immediately practical concerns — directing you to the nearest gas station or to the closest inexpensive Chinese restaurant, or finding you a bed for the night. And it could tell you what's on and what's open in your immediate neighborhood.

Silicon-smart vehicles can also calculate efficient routes from their current locations to specified destinations. Finding the shortest path through a street network is a straightforward software task (though doing so efficiently can get a bit tricky when the network is large), and whatever information is available about current traffic conditions can be factored in. The chosen route might simply be displayed on a dashboard screen, but it can almost as easily be output as a sequence of instructions from a robotic back-seat driver — "Next left," "You just made a wrong turn," and so on. Integration of some simple speech-recognition capabilities can even allow the driver to ask "What now?"

Not only may vehicles sense where they are in the road system, but the road system may also be equipped with electronic sensors enabling it to detect where the vehicles are. So the old ideas of the tollbooth and the on-ramp meter can be updated; charges for the use of a road can, in principle, be adjusted instantaneously according to the level of road congestion.[35] The task of the smart vehicle then becomes not just one of calculating the shortest or quickest path to a specified destination, but of computing the cheapest path or of finding a reasonably quick route that does not cost too much. In the future, travel through cities will involve continuous information exchange between smart vehicles and smart roadway systems.[36]

As I contemplate all this, I recall Roy Rogers and Trigger — an all-terrain vehicle with abundant onboard intelligence. Trigger always knew where he was, could find his way home if necessary, and understood moment-by-moment what his master needed; horse and cowboy functioned as one. But when the horse vanished from everyday life, leaving behind the horseless carriage, the onboard intelligence went too; there was a technological gap to be filled. (Roy obviously didn't have quite the same relationship to his jeep.) Increasingly, now, electronics are doing the job. Soon, our automobiles will be at least as smart as Trigger, and the car-and-driver relationship will return to the cowpoke-and-horseflesh mode. And when they get smarter still, the horseless carriage may evolve into the driverless automobile.

As a result, we are beginning to know and use cities in new ways. Long ago the urban theorist Kevin Lynch pointed out the fundamental relationship between human cognition and urban form — the importance of the learned mental maps that knowledgeable locals carry about inside their skulls. These mental maps, together with the landmarks and edges that provide orientation within the urban fabric, are what make a city seem familiar and comprehensible. But for us artificially intelligent cyborgs, the ability to navigate through the streets and gain access to a city's resources isn't all in our heads. Increasingly, we rely on our electronic extensions — smart vehicles and hand-held devices, together with the invisible landmarks provided by electronic positioning systems — to orient us in the urban fabric, to capture and process knowledge of our surroundings, and to get us to where we want to go.

BEING THERE

For millennia architects have been concerned with the skin-bounded body and its immediate sensory environment — with providing shelter, warmth, and safety, with casting light on the surfaces that surround it, with creating conditions for conversation and music, with orchestrating the touch of hard and soft and rough and smooth materials, and with breezes and scents. Now they must contemplate electronically augmented, reconfigurable, virtual bodies that can sense and act at a distance but that also remain partially anchored in their immediate surroundings. (The *Neuromancer* fantasy of cyberspace that totally masks physical space — and so produces completely disembodied electronic existence — represents a theoretical limit, not a practical condition.)

When you wear your Walkman on the bus, your feet are on the floor and your eyes see the physical enclosure, but an electronic audio environment masks the immediately surrounding one and your ears are in another place. When you don a head-mounted stereo display to play *Dactyl Nightmare* in a virtual reality arcade, the immediate visual environment is supplanted by virtual space, but your sense of touch reminds you that you still remain surrounded by now-invisible solid objects. When you juxtapose a videoconference window to a distant time zone with a glazed opening to the immediate surroundings, you can contrast night with day and winter with summer. Increasingly the architectures of physical space and cyberspace — of the specifically situated body and of its fluid electronic extensions — are superimposed, intertwined, and hybridized in complex ways. The classical unities of architectural space and experience have shattered — as the dramatic unities long ago fragmented on the stage — and architects now need to design for this new condition.

As we look back to previous eras, we multiply augmented cyborgs can recognize that we have much to be thankful for. But we should not forget our roots — the cultures of those long, pre-silicon centuries in which our ancestors had to do it all with protoplasm. They had little opportunity to extend their nervous systems or upgrade their bodies, so they made places for inhabitation — buildings and cities — that were carefully fitted to the scale and limitations of the original equipment and structured to promote constant face-to-face, eye-to-eye, within earshot and within arm's length contact.

Life in pre-cyborg places was a very different experience. You really had to be there.

4

The first building provides a physical space to assemble: Viollet-le-Duc's speculation from 1876.

Telepresence creates a virtual space to assemble: a *Punch* cartoonist's speculation from 1878,

As our bodies morph into cyborgs, the buildings that house them are also transforming. Increasingly, telecommunication systems replace circulation systems, and the solvent of digital information decomposes traditional building types. One by one, the familiar forms vanish. Then the residue of recombinant fragments yields up mutants.

FACADE / INTERFACE

First, some historical perspective. Not so long ago, when the world seemed simpler, buildings corresponded one-to-one with institutions and rendered those institutions visible. Architecture played an

RECOMBINANT ARCHITECTURE

indispensable representational role by providing occupations, organizations, and social groupings with their public faces. Firehouses were for firefighters, schoolhouses were for scholars, and jailhouses were for jailbirds. The monarch's palace at Versailles, like the Forbidden City of Beijing or the Red Fort in Delhi, housed the ruler and his court, and its in-your-face form unambiguously expressed established power; it was where the ruling got done, and it was what you tried to grab if you wanted to usurp. Everyone knew that the General Motors headquarters building in Detroit — with its boardroom on the topmost floor — was where cigar-sucking captains of industry ran the company and decided (so they thought) what was good for the country as well. Buildings were distinguished from one another by their differing uses, and the inventory of those uses represented social division and structure. The Roman theorist Vitruvius recognized this when he enunciated the principle of architectural decorum — appropriateness of form to purpose and status. And when the French revolutionary architect Ledoux wanted to demonstrate the possibility of a new social order, he designed and drew the hardware of his utopia — *architecture parlante,* the buildings that were to accommodate and vividly illustrate its restructured institutions.

Under this historically familiar condition, the internal organization of a building — its subdivision into parts, the interrelation of those parts by the circulation system, and the evident hierarchies of privacy and control — reflected the structure of the institution and physically diagrammed its pattern of activities. There was a complementarity of life and bricks and mortar, like that of snail and shell. If there was a mismatch, then the building had to be modified or the institution was forced to adapt. In his best Obi wan-Kenobi mode, remarking on the British Houses of Parliament, Winston Churchill cast this point into a much-quoted aphorism: we make our buildings and our buildings make us.[1]

But now, increasingly, software beats hardware. In the early 1990s, for example, Columbia University scrapped plans to build a twenty-million-dollar addition to its law library and instead bought a Connection Machine (a state-of-the-art supercomputer) and embarked on a program of scanning and storing ten thousand deteriorating old books yearly.[2] Library users would no longer go to a card catalogue and then physically retrieve books from the stacks. Nor would they open books, look up topics of interest in the table of contents or the index, and then flip through the pages to get to what they wanted. At computer workstations, they would enter queries (in plain English), retrieve lists of stored documents in response, and search through those documents to find relevant passages.[3] The task of designing and implementing the library extension had been fundamentally redefined. It was no longer one of laying out and constructing a building, with storage and circulation areas, to house the shelf space required by an expanding collection. It became one of designing and programming the computer tools for storing, querying, retrieving, and displaying digitally encoded text. Henceforth, the library would be extensible and reconfigurable in software.

Today, institutions generally are supported not only by buildings and their furnishings, but also by telecommunication systems and computer software. And the digital, electronic, virtual side is increasingly taking over from the physical. In many contexts, storage of bits is displacing storage of physical artifacts such as books, so that the need for built space is reduced. Electronic linkage is substituting for physical accessibility and for convenient connection by the internal circulation systems of buildings, so that access imperatives no longer play such powerful roles in clustering and organizing architectural spaces. And — as when an ATM screen rather than a door in a neoclassical edifice on Main Street provides access to a bank — computer-generated graphic displays are replacing built facades as the public faces of institutions.

It is time to update Churchill's *bon mot.* Now we make our *networks* and our networks make us.

B o o k s t o r e s   /   B i t s t o r e s

The most obvious epicenter of this shakeup is the information business. And it is particularly instructive to consider the fate of one of its most familiar architectural manifestations, the book shop. Where will we find twenty-first-century Pickwicks?

The problem with printed books, magazines, and newspapers — Gutenberg's gotcha — is distribution. Paper documents can be mass produced rapidly at centralized locations, but they must then be warehoused, transported, stocked at retail outlets, and eventually hand carried to wherever they will be opened and read. There are built and specially equipped places for each of these activities: the publisher's office, the printing plant, the warehouse, the bookstore, the newspaper kiosk, lounges and waiting rooms stocked with magazines, and the easy chair beside the fire. These places are distributed at appropriate locations within the urban fabric and play important roles in differentiating that fabric and the activities unfolding within it. Harvard Square would not be the same without Out of Town News and its diverse collection of bookstores.

Records and videos generate analogous places and spatial structures. The record store long ago took its place alongside the bookstore in downtown retail districts and shopping malls. Then, in the 1980s, video stores popped up everywhere — proliferating particularly in strips, shopping centers, and rural market centers, where they could easily be reached by car. Like the gas station and the fast-food outlet, video stores became a characteristic element of the suburban landscape.

When we separate information from its usual paper and plastic substrates, though, stockpiling and transporting physical products become unnecessary. Consider, for example, a venture announced by Blockbuster Entertainment (a large video-rental and record store chain) and IBM in May 1993.[4] The idea was to store recordings, in digital format, on a central server and to distribute them via a computer network to kiosks in record stores. There, customers could select recordings from a menu, download them to the kiosk, and copy them to CDs on the spot. Bookstores could work the same way, by downloading texts and rapidly laser-printing them. Through such point-of-sale production, the producers and wholesalers save on inventory, warehouse, and transportation costs, the retailers save on shelf space, and the customer potentially gets access to a much wider selection.

But inscription on to the substrate need not necessarily occur at this particular point along the information distribution chain. (Though, naturally enough, it is the point that most interests retailers.) Electronic, digital distribution might carry all the way to homes or other points of consumption. An alternative publishing strategy, then, is to download books and magazines from online databases to home laser printers (successors to the crude fax machines of the 1980s and 1990s) and to download recordings to home stereos, videos to home televisions, and newspapers to home computers. (This can be integrated with a recycling strategy; print on recycled paper and toss the printouts back into the recycling bin when their useful life is over.) Yet another strategy for text, music, or video on demand is simply to provide hundreds or thousands of simultaneously available digital channels, with each one repeatedly broadcasting specialized programs.

The Internet's Electronic Newsstand pioneered the new publishing pattern of downloading on demand when it opened in July 1993.[5] It provided online access to magazine articles — thus allowing customers to browse, as they might in a traditional newsstand — and also allowed convenient placement of subscription orders for print versions. An electronic bookstore and sections for business publications and newsletters were soon added. It was established with eight magazines; less than a year later the list had grown to eighty, and the service was being accessed forty thousand times per day from all over the world.

With changes in modes of information distribution come changes in acts of consumption — even in the familiar ritual of reading a newspaper. As I write this, the *New York Times* and the *Boston Globe* — in the form of large lumps of reprocessed cellulose — land with thumps on my Cambridge doorstep each morning and must eventually find their way to the recycling bin. The *Chicago Tribune,* the *San Jose Mercury News,* and many others show up as well, but silently and immaterially — on my computer. Instead of turning their pages, I use software that picks out the items I want to see; headlines become menu items to click. Or I can do keyword searches through databases of accumulated stories. It's a short step to the completely personalized newspaper produced by an interface agent that knows my interests and preferences, continually scans the incoming news stream to pick out items that match my interest profile, and displays them in whatever format I may happen to prefer. Even the ideas of a "daily paper" and a self-contained "story" are challenged; a newspaper can become an accumulating online database of news stories in which a current story is simply an entry point for tracing a topic back through previous stories.

By the mid-1990s a new pattern of information distribution was clearly emerging on the North American continent. Cable, telephone, and computer companies were scrambling to form alliances that would provide homes and workplaces with inexpensive network connections, processing hardware, and presentation software. In 1993, for example, Time Warner announced an ambitious test project to put inexpensive telecomputers in four thousand homes in Orlando, Florida, and the Videoway network in Montreal was already offering a commercially successful interactive television system.[6] Media biggie Rupert Murdoch began to buy into the Internet.[7] Publishers were starting to evolve into organizations that pumped bits into the Net — the loading docks of the information superhighway system. The growing expectation was that bookstores, record stores, video stores, lending libraries, and newspaper kiosks in urban centers would largely be replaced by millions of inconspicuous, widely distributed electronic boxes at the ends of cables.

Gutenberg's revolution created places where printed information was concentrated and controlled. But electronic, digital information has a radically different spatial logic. It is immaterial rather than bonded to paper or plastic sheets, it is almost instantaneously transferable to any place that has a network connection or is within range of a bit radiation source, and it is potentially reprocessable at any reception point — thus shifting much of the editorial and formatting work and responsibility from the producer's centralized plant to the consumer's personal hardware and software. Even more importantly, elimination of the need for access to printing presses and paper supplies has removed traditional barriers to entering the publishing business; anyone with an inexpensive computer and a network connection can now set up a server and pump out bits.

The likely result is a radical change in the sizes and locations of information supply points. When the Chicago Tribune Tower was constructed, it stood as the proudly visible center of a vast collection and distribution system and an emblem of the power of the press. Every day the news flowed in and the printed papers flowed out to the surrounding metropolis. But on the infobahn, where every node is potentially both a publication and consumption point, such centralized concentrations of activity will be supplanted by millions of dispersed fragments.

STACKS / SERVERS

The old British Museum reading room provided an architectural interface to the vast book stacks that lay beyond. From outside, the classical, columnar facade functioned as an icon — signifier of an access point. From within the circular, domed reading room (which looks in plan like a sectored hard disk), books could be summoned up by the action of specifying a call number. Library attendants would then retrieve volumes from the stacks for use at a reading table. (In later years, tourists would come to look for the very table at which Karl Marx sat absorbing vast amounts of printed information and transforming it into a blueprint for revolution.) The cycle would be completed by performing the task of reshelving the books

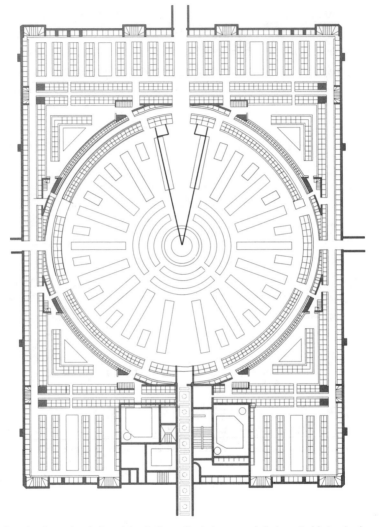

Iron book stacks designed by Anthony Panizzi surround Sydney Smirke's circular, domed reading room at the British Museum library, London (1854–56).

until they were needed again. Functionally, the whole thing was a very large, very slow version of what computer technicians now know as a database server: you send requests, and you get back items of stored information.

This highly refined functional diagram was the outcome of a long evolutionary process.[8] In early libraries, with small numbers of volumes, books had lined the walls of the reading room. Later, as the ratio of book storage to reading space changed, the book stacks were separated from the reading rooms and increasingly became the dominant spatial element; the new type was clearly emerging in Leopoldo della Santa's 1816 theoretical project for a library.[9] By the time that Karl Friedrich Schinkel produced his Berlin Staatsbibliothek project in 1835–36, it seemed logical to propose a huge, rectangular block of gridded stack space with a grand public stair in the center and access stairs at the four corners. And in 1854–56, when Sydney Smirke designed his rotunda for insertion into the older fabric of the British Museum, the book stacks became a huge, separate iron structure.

Popular graphical user interfaces of personal computers function in much the same way as Smirke's careful architectural arrangements. Icons are arrayed on the screen, like doorways along a street, to make visible the available access points. Clicking on an icon (like knocking on a door) puts the user in a space — in this case a rectangular "window" on the screen — from which files of information can be requested. In response to user requests, software routines retrieve files from the disk, display them on the screen for inspection and manipulation, and perhaps eventually rewrite them back to the disk.

Now extrapolate from this small-scale example and imagine a 10-million-volume, digital, online, humanities research library.[10] (For comparison, the Library of Congress had nearly 15 million volumes on 550 miles of shelves in the early 1990s, the British Library had about 12 million on a couple of hundred miles, and Harvard's Widener had about 3.5 million.)[11] The catalogue would be available on the network. Volumes or chapters might be downloaded to a scholar's personal workstation in a minute or two, then displayed or laser-printed as required. (It matters little where the digital volumes physically reside — just that they can be accessed efficiently — and they occupy little physical space anyway. The collection's existence would not be celebrated architecturally, as the grandiose mass of Widener celebrates the accumulative power of Harvard.) This library would never close. Those addicted to the look and feel of tree flakes encased in dead cow (and prepared to pay for it) would not have to kick the habit; elegant physical volumes could automatically be generated on demand. Nothing would ever be checked out, in somebody else's carrel, lost, or in the limbo of the reshelving cart. Old volumes could live out their days in safe and dignified retirement in climate-controlled book museums. And the librarians could run backups (look what happened to the Library of Alexandria, where they didn't have a way to do it!).

The task facing the designers of this soft library is a transformation (with some invariants, but many radical changes) of what faced the Smirke brothers and the librarian Panizzi as they evolved the design for the British Museum and Library.[12] The facade is not to be constructed of stone and located on a street in Bloomsbury, but of pixels on thousands of screens scattered throughout the world. Organizing book stacks and providing access to them turns into a task of structuring a database and providing search and retrieval routines. Reading tables become display windows on screens. Resources are made available to the public by allowing anyone to log in and by providing computer workstations in public places, rather than by opening reading room doors. The huge stacks shrink to

almost negligible size, the seats and carrels disperse, and there is
nothing left to put a grand facade *on*.

It will not be possible to tell tourists where some Marx of the next
millennium sat. All that is solid melts in air.

GALLERIES / VIRTUAL MUSEUMS

Art galleries and museums arrange exhibits in carefully constructed
viewing sequences. At blockbuster shows, the long lines of visitors
shuffle from one item to the next.

Designing a great museum, then, has traditionally been a task of
relating wall or cabinet display space, with appropriate natural
lighting, to a circulation system that efficiently conducts visitors
through the collection.[13] Nineteenth-century neoclassicists typically solved the problem by symmetrically arranging long, rectangular, skylit gallery spaces around grand, central entrance halls;
visitors would enter and orient themselves, circulate around the
perimeter, and eventually return to the starting point. The great
examples are Leo von Klenze's Glyptothek and Alte Pinakothek in
Munich and Schinkel's Altes Museum in Berlin. (At the brilliantly
planned Pinakothek, parallel galleries are cross-connected so that
visitors can depart from the perimeter circulation ring at will.) But
there are other alternatives: at the Guggenheim in New York,
Frank Lloyd Wright twisted a single, continuous gallery into a helix
wrapped around a skylit atrium. Here, visitors take an elevator to
the top and then descend along the ramped floor.

Within such arrangements, the curatorial task is to order exhibits
into meaningful sequences. In the Glyptothek works of sculpture
have traditionally been set out chronologically — beginning with
Egypt, progressing through Greece and Rome, and ending with
moderns like Canova. In the painting galleries of the Altes Museum

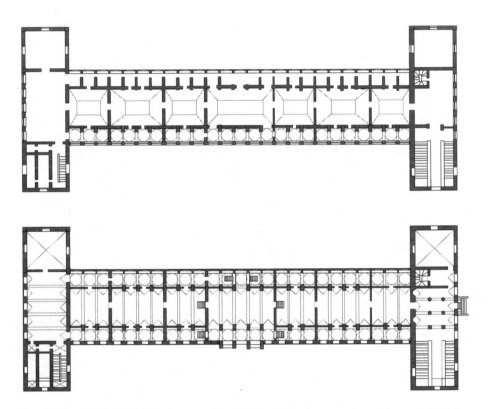

The Alte Pinakothek, Munich, by Leo von Klenze (1826–36). On the upper floor, interconnected halls were designed to display the works of different schools in chronological sequence.

there was a carefully constructed progression of "quality," leading up to the "perfection" of the High Renaissance. And in the Pinakothek arrangement was by "schools" in roughly chronological order: Flemish, German, French, Spanish, and Italian. Natural history museums, responding to different intellectual agendas, usually arranged exhibits according to scientific principles — by taxonomic grouping, in evolutionary sequence, or by geographic origin. Though older museums and galleries were often designed to present unchanging collections in fixed sequences, this need not be the case; their more modern equivalents usually provide flexible spaces for installing temporary shows.

In a virtual museum digital images of paintings, videos of living organisms, or three-dimensional simulations of sculptures and works of architecture (perhaps destroyed or unbuilt ones) stand in for physical objects, and a temporal sequence on the display plays the role of a spatial sequence along a circulation path. This yields tremendous spatial compression; a huge collection can be viewed, exhibit by exhibit, on a personal computer or in a small video theater. Sprawling gallery spaces become unnecessary.

Crowds become easy to handle. The exhibit material is kept on servers on a network, and viewers can be scattered at remote locations. It is not gallery capacity that matters, but server capability and network bandwidth.

Arrangement and sequencing of material remain crucial issues, of course, but the solutions to the problem are implemented in software instead of being built inflexibly and irrevocably into bricks-and-mortar constructions. Each item in the collection can have hyperlinks to other items that are related in some interesting way, so that the virtual museum visitor can construct a particular path through the collection according to personal interest. A virtual museum can offer far more choices for exploration than even the Pinakothek.

As virtual museums develop, the role of actual museums will shift; they will increasingly be seen as places for going back to the originals. The diagram is clear in the new Sainsbury wing of London's National Gallery. Near the entrance there is a room called the Micro Gallery, containing computer workstations from which visitors can explore the entire collection in hypermedia form.[14] As they do so, visitors note items they will want to see in the original. At the conclusion of the virtual tour, they get a printed plan for a correspondingly personalized tour of the actual museum. An overlay of virtual space thus changes the use of the actual space.

THEATERS / ENTERTAINMENT INFRASTRUCTURE

Entertainment is information. Actors, directors, singers, and dancers produce it. Audiences consume it. Theaters distribute it. That's the crude analysis, anyway.

Ancient Greek and Roman theaters were compact, elegant distribution diagrams. Since an unaided actor's voice cannot carry very far, spectators were packed in tight circles around the point of production. And, since unobstructed lines of sight were essential, these circles were raked. The audience could see and hear the actors, the actors could see and hear the audience, and the whole system was wrapped up into a neat architectural package.

Andrea Palladio's late-sixteenth-century Teatro Olimpico in Vicenza (among others of around the same time) brought the circles of seats in under a weather-tight roof and got very sophisticated about the sightlines. Two centuries later, in Giuseppe Piermarini's design for La Scala in Milan, the seats were augmented (as

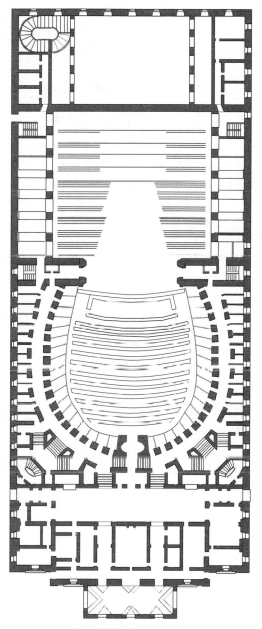

Teatro alla Scala, Milan, by Giuseppe Piermarini (1776–78). The auditorium is configured to keep audience members within earshot of the performers and to provide them with clear views of the stage.

had become customary in Europe) by vertically stacked circles of private boxes — a lot of little drawing rooms with the fourth walls removed, as Proust shrewdly described them.[15]

Broadcast media (radio and television) enlarged the spectator circles to encompass entire communities and shattered the once-unified audience space into thousands of scattered armchairs, couches, car seats, boom-box emplacements, and ear-to-ear spans of head-phones. Proust's drawing rooms now spun out of their fixed orbits; recall how the film *American Graffiti* evoked a soft theater centered on the local radio tower — a radiation field emanating from Wolf-man Jack, engulfing the ranch-house living rooms and cruising automobiles of a 1950s California town. Transmission towers re-placed stage towers, and invisible circles of pulsing electromagnetic waves supplanted static arcs of spectator seating. Since audiences grew huge, broadcast studios became (as Frankfurt School com-mentators observed, with vivid anxiety about the consequences) favored platforms for big-time manipulators of public opinion — advertisers, demagogues, talk-show hosts, and televangelists.[16]

Electronic enlargement of the spectator circles had an additional important consequence; since performers could no longer hear their far-flung audiences laughing, groaning, muttering, hissing, heckling, cheering, and clapping, the flow of information became almost entirely unidirectional. The traditional asymmetry of theat-rical performance was vastly exaggerated. Direct engagement of performers and audiences disappeared, to be replaced partially and unsatisfactorily (if at all) by expedients such as studio audiences, telephone call-ins, and Nielsen boxes.

But switched, broadband, two-way cable networks of the kind that were under development by the early 1990s — sophisticated bit-distribution utilities, much like the water, gas, sewage, and electrical systems which have become so fundamental to modern cities — transform this condition. Most obviously, they can be hooked up to large video servers that allow subscribers interactively to select videos from extensive menus, play them whenever they want, and operate a "virtual VCR" to control viewing conditions. It's "video on demand," as its promoters have dubbed it.

But the traditionally structured video does not have to be the unit that is retrieved and played; finer-grained interactions with hypermedia entertainment productions also become possible. Early versions of these sorts of productions first became popular in the personal computer era, and initially were distributed on floppy disk or CD; in the early 1990s there was an initial flurry of interest in branching hypertext novels with multithreaded narrative structures that could be followed in many different ways, and there were a few experiments with larger-scale hypertext fictions on the Internet. There was also some experimentation with "branching" movies in specially equipped theaters. As switched broadband networks bring sufficient bandwidth into living rooms to allow interactive video, and as home audiences become large enough to justify expensive productions, interactive productions seem destined to become the norm rather than the exception.

Live performances — broadcast, narrowcast, or point-to-point — can also become interactive. You might, for example, have a very literal kind of virtual auditorium in which the display screen functions as a stage and your remote has buttons for sending back applause and other codified responses. If you receive three-dimensional models of a sporting event rather than a stream of two-dimensional video images, you could take control of some directorial functions by selecting viewpoints and operating a virtual camera. It surely will not be very long before there are two-way video equivalents of talk radio. And, no doubt, there will be virtual 47th

Streets and "combat zones" to provide an endless variety of private sexual performances on demand; as 900 numbers, Minitel, and X-rated chat rooms have amply demonstrated, skilled performers can easily overcome bandwidth and interface limitations.

Competitive games will be reinvented for virtual arenas. The usual way to set up a game has been to bring small numbers of competitors together in precisely marked physical places — over chessboards, on tennis courts, basketball courts, or football fields — while spectators watch from the sidelines. In 1993 the hack-and-slash hit *Doom* effectively exploited the idea of putting networked participants together in *virtual* places to battle software monsters and to duel with each other. And by 1994 the videogame pioneer Nolan Bushnell was speculating about the possibility of network-supported, intercity competitive games involving tens of thousands of participants on each team.[17]

Carried to their logical conclusion, these reconfigurations and transformations completely rip apart the traditional architectural relationship between stage and auditorium, performers and audience. The great house of the theater condenses into an electronic box with a screen and a video camera. When you want to be a spectator, the bezel of the screen becomes your proscenium — framer of the action. When you want to become an actor, the camera provides access to an audience and the entire network is potentially your auditorium. And when you want to be a game participant, the network allows you to meet teammates and opponents on virtual turf.

Not only has the old idea of concentrated, physically coherent theatrical or competition space been subverted and eroded, so has that of performance time. Early "live" radio and television shows carefully preserved the theatrical convention of definite performance time, but programmers soon learned tricks of repeating and time-shifting recorded performances and of mixing live and re-corded material. With the development of networked interactive video, the show goes on anytime anybody wants it to.

All this reshapes the rules of production and distribution. Under traditional arrangements, the cost of getting to an audience tends to be high; a show has to fill expensive theater seats or attract sufficient advertising to pay for production costs and air time. So the entertainment industry has increasingly become a game for very big players who compete for mass audiences. But as high-band-width networks proliferate, and as network navigation software grows in sophistication, the costs of reaching and aggregating audi-ences should diminish sharply. There will be opportunities to pro-duce and distribute low-budget entertainment for very small audiences and to identify and reach scattered audiences with the most specialized of interests and tastes. The infobahn may become a vast, global Broadway lined with thousands of virtual theaters.

So the social superglue of necessary proximity between performers and audience is losing its old stickiness, and the traditional archi-tectural types and social conventions (going to the theater, cheering for your local team in the ballpark) that we associate with perfor-mance are coming unstuck. Speech, music, scenes, and text can now be transmuted into bits and entered into the network almost anywhere. These bits can be decoded to create a performance wherever and whenever a spectator chooses to plug in. Established distinctions between producers and consumers of entertainment (reified by the forms of theater and stadium construction) are breaking down. Soon, all the world will be an electronic stage.

S C H O O L H O U S E S / V I R T U A L C A M P U S E S

A teacher speaks; students listen and respond. The teacher has access to some corpus of knowledge, beliefs, and practices, and makes this

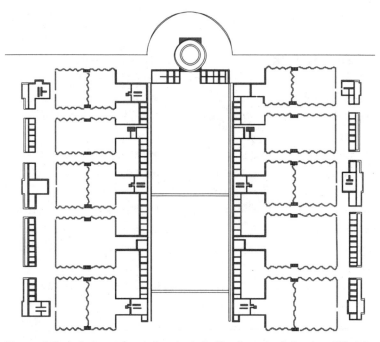

Thomas Jefferson's layout for an "academical village" — the University of Virginia, Charlottesville (1817–26). Rooms for students and instructors, and meeting places of various kinds, are linked by colonnaded cloisters.

corpus available to the students. Schools, colleges, and universities are spaces that exist primarily to bring students and teachers together so that this sharing of a corpus can take place.

The underlying diagram of a school appears in its simplest and most beautiful form when disciples gather within earshot of a guru in a place made by the shade of a bo tree.[18] The less sedentary Socrates strolled in a grove, with his disciples keeping pace. The little red schoolhouse — appropriate to colder climates — puts the students in a box with the teacher in front. Jeremy Bentham's proposed "Chrestomathic" monitorial school — a variant on the panopticon — had a single master in the middle surrounded by a circle of six monitors to keep order, then circular tiers with seats for nine hundred boys.[19]

Modern schools, colleges, and universities have greater spatial differentiation and far more complex plans. They provide multiple classrooms to allow different sorts of instruction to proceed simultaneously; they add libraries, laboratories, art and design studios, music practice rooms, and other specialized facilities; and they link the pieces together with long cloisters or passageways (MIT's "infinite corridor" is emblematic). Residential institutions — like that planned by Thomas Jefferson at the University of Virginia — integrate rooms for scholars and provide hierarchies of informal and formal meeting places, so that the plan reads as an illustration of the dedicated scholarly life. The demand that colleges and universities typically make is to be "in residence" — to be part of the spatially defined community. And these communities enforce, as well, strict compliance with academic timetables, classroom schedules, and calendars.

Of course there have always been alternatives to making such permanent, rigidly organized places of learning. Preindustrial societies had their itinerant teachers and holy men who spread the word wherever they could find audiences. By providing printed books and efficient mail service, the Industrial Revolution made correspondence schools possible. Two-way radio allowed a teacher in Alice Springs to instruct children living on remote cattle stations scattered across the great Australian outback. In the era of the Wilson government, broadcast television and videotapes (in conjunction with reasonably good, old-fashioned mail service) created the possibility of Britain's Open University. Today digital telecommunication is producing a powerful resurgence of this alternative tradition; being online may soon become a more important mark of community membership than being in residence. (When the Aga Khan gave MIT's commencement address in 1994, he was not given the traditional honorary degree to make him symbolically part of the community, but rather a modem-equipped laptop computer and an MIT e-mail address.)

As the digital telecommunications era dawned, some universities were very quick to begin exploring the potential role of campus networks. At Dartmouth in the 1960s — way back in the era of time-sharing mainframes — a network of interactive terminals was put in place and heavily used.[20] At MIT in the 1980s, with extensive support from IBM and Digital, the campus-wide Athena system pioneered the educational use of networked workstations with (by the standards of the time) high-bandwidth interconnections.[21] By the 1990s campus networks were commonplace; even the ivy-clad dorms in Harvard Yard had been hooked up.

At the same time (beginning in the 1970s), ARPANET, BITNET, and ultimately the Internet began to shake up the traditional, insular structures of colleges and universities by creating quick, convenient, inexpensive channels for worldwide, campus-to-campus interchange of text and data. These long-distance links were hooked up to local networks, such as MIT's Athena, which disseminated access around the campuses themselves. Scholars quickly found that electronic contact with distant correspondents could sometimes be more rewarding than conversation with colleagues from just down the hall. Online conferences and bulletin boards began to challenge departmental common rooms and local hangouts as the best places to pick up the latest on specialized topics. By the 1990s many academics found that they simultaneously inhabited local scholarly communities, which provided their offices and paid their salaries, and virtual communities, which supplied much of their intellectual nourishment and made increasing demands on their time and loyalties. The tension was beginning to show.

Network connections quickly create new ways of sharing knowledge and enacting practices and so force changes in the characters of teaching spaces. At the very least, a lecture theater now needs a computer workstation integrated with the podium and a computer-connected video projector to supplement the old blackboards and slide projectors; the podium is no longer a place for reading from a book or lecturing from written notes, but a spot for directing and interpreting a stream of bits. And instead of taking notes on paper, students use their laptop computers to capture and annotate these bits.

Seminar rooms change too. They now need to be set up for videoconferencing as well as for face-to-face discussions.[22] But that is just the beginning. Desktop-to-desktop, switched video networks open the more radical possibility of teaching in virtual rather than traditional physical settings. Students might have office conferences with faculty members without leaving their dormitory rooms. Seminars might be conducted without seminar rooms. Symposia might virtually assemble speakers from widely scattered locations. Lecturers might perform from distant places, and without the need to concentrate students in auditoriums.

School and university libraries become less like document warehouses and dispensaries and more like online information-brokering services. Reserve desks are supplanted by online document collections, and slide libraries by huge image and video-on-demand servers. Centralized reading rooms fragment into scattered information access points; any place where a student or faculty member may want to sit and work — an auditorium seat, library carrel, desk, dorm room, or office — needs a laptop hookup point.

Even laboratories can sometimes be broken up and scattered — and benefit from it.[23] The Harvard-Smithsonian Center for Astrophysics, for example, has developed an astronomical system called MicroObservatory. The master units of this system are networked computers in school classrooms. These are used to control motorized, digital-imaging telescopes mounted on rooftops and to view the telescope images remotely. Image-processing software is used to subtract out the sky so that observations can be made in the daytime. An extended version of this system might incorporate hundreds of telescopes scattered around the world and allow students to make observations from anywhere there is a network connection.

As the twentieth century draws to a close, the idea of a virtual campus — paralleling or perhaps replacing the physical one — seems increasingly plausible.[24] If a latter-day Jefferson were to lay out an ideal educational community for the third millennium, she might site it in cyberspace.

HOSPITALS / TELEMEDICINE

The word "hospital" derives from the Latin *hospes,* meaning guest or host; the idea is to confine the sick to one place.[25] In early monastic hospitals the sick were confined so that they could be cared for by the monks and (perhaps more to the point, considering the level of medical treatment that was available) so that they could conveniently be assembled for religious services and speeded on their way to heaven; thus Filarete's famous plan for the Ospedale Maggiore in Milan consisted of immense cruciform wards with

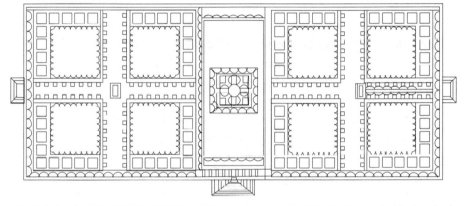

Intended plan for the Ospedale Maggiore, Milan, as shown in Filarete's *Treatise on Architecture* (early 1460s). Cruciform wards, with altars at the crossings, flank a chapel in the central courtyard.

altars at the crossings and a chapel in the central courtyard. (In modern wards the centrally located altars are replaced by nursing stations.) Sometimes, as in hospitals for infectious diseases like Venice's island *lazaretto* and in asylums for the mentally ill like Bedlam and Charenton, the sick have been confined to keep them away from the rest of society. As medical expertise and increasingly sophisticated medical technology have developed in the twentieth century, confinement has been to places where skilled practitioners, medical records, and advanced facilities (such as surgical suites, pathology laboratories, and medical imaging installations) could be concentrated. And in teaching hospitals, the sick are assembled in places where students can observe them.

Before Pasteur, enlightened hospital designers arranged long, narrow wards to provide as much external wall surface, natural light, and fresh air as possible. So, for example, both Wren's early-eighteenth-century plan for the Royal Naval Hospital at Greenwich and Durand's ideal hospital plan of a century later are low, sprawling, symmetrical accretions of ward pavilions, courtyards, and immensely lengthy corridors.[26] But since the 1870s, when Pasteur fingered bacteria (rather than foul air) as the agents of infection and Lister developed antiseptic medicine, pavilions have become a thing of the past. Twentieth-century hospitals consist mostly of air-conditioned, artificially lit spaces packed closely together in deep, multistoried blocks to minimize staff, patient movement, and service system runs. The hospital designer's task — much like the task of microprocessor chip layout — has been to arrange a lot of identical storage units and a few specialized, central processing facilities for the greatest possible circulation efficiency under statistically predicted patterns of use.[27] Generally, the resulting places have not been very pleasant.

With the development of advanced telecommunications, bits are now beginning to transform hospital design as profoundly as bacteria once did. Telemedicine is emerging. It brings advanced medical care to widely scattered populations and makes old-style assemblies of patients around specialized medical facilities less necessary. As John McConnell, writing in *The Lancet*, summarized, "For any procedure that involves vision or sound (e.g., monitoring the progress of anaesthesia, or giving an opinion on a biopsy slide, fetal ultrasound, or computed tomography scan) — and potentially even touch — the physician need no longer be present in the same room, or even in the same country, as the patient or specimen."[28]

The simplest and most obvious form of telemedicine is a straightforward extension of teleconferencing. Using video hookups, specialists at major medical centers can examine patients and provide advice to colleagues in remote rural locations. Emergency room physicians can save precious time by examining patients in video-equipped ambulances, and military hospital medics can examine far-off wounded. Where outbreaks of fighting or natural disasters create sudden demands for medical care, capacity can quickly be switched from other parts of the world. Basic models of health care delivery may even begin to change; family practitioners might provide face-to-face patient contact while drawing on the expertise of distant specialists by video as needed. By the 1990s, then, numerous experiments in video-based telemedicine were under way.[29]

But video is only the first step. Since modern diagnostic devices often produce streams of digital data, they can readily be adapted to provide their output remotely through network connections. So stethoscopes, otoscopes, endoscopes, electrocardiography devices, and medical imaging machines can all now be used in remote examinations. As homes get network connections, domestic diagnostic and monitoring devices will begin to allow virtual house calls; when your baby has an earache, you might connect to a virtual clinic and put the otoscope in the baby's ear to let the practitioner on duty take a look.[30] It's not as good as a real visit, perhaps, but it's a lot better than a telephone call.

By combining electronic viewing and diagnostic devices with appropriate telemanipulators, medical practitioners can begin to make themselves telepresent.[31] Consider, for example, a pathologist examining tissue samples or body fluids under a microscope in order to render a diagnosis; with a telepathology system consisting of a video camera mounted on a motorized microscope, this task can be performed remotely.[32] And with fancier teleoperators, head-mounted stereo displays, and sufficiently precise tactile feedback devices, telesurgery becomes a serious possibility.[33] A typical telesurgery system consists of master and slave units: the remotely located surgeon wears a helmet (the audiovisual master) that controls a stereo video camera (audiovisual slave) observing the surgery, and holds force-reflecting pseudotools that control a surgical robot.[34]

Continuous care — involving constant monitoring and regular medication — might also be provided remotely. (Many of the necessary technologies were originally developed for battlefield use but can readily be adapted for more peaceful purposes.)[35] Houses and beds can contain sensors for tracking the conditions of their occupants and telecommunications for transmitting the information to distant monitoring sites. Electronic scales can log body weight. Noncontact, microwave vital-signs monitoring systems can measure heart rate, respiration rate, temperature, and blood pressure. Smart air-conditioning systems and inquisitive toilets might automatically take samples and perform analyses. Implanted wireless devices might be used for remotely controlled release of precise amounts of medication. Houses seem destined to evolve into increasingly sophisticated components of health care systems.

One promise of telemedicine is that the isolated, the immobilized, and those in sudden, acute need will be able to get care without difficult and time-consuming travel. Another is that family practitioners and paramedics who have direct contact with patients will be able to draw more effectively on specialized expertise and advanced medical technology as the traditional doctor's black bag mutates into a sophisticated digital telecommunications device. An obvious peril is that health care delivery may become an even more depersonalized and technocratic process. Either way, the logic of health care facility location and internal organization is changing dramatically; whereas the industrial, antiseptic care, and medical technology revolutions of the nineteenth and early twentieth centuries created powerful incentives to centralize medical care and concentrate it in major urban areas, the digital telecommunications revolution of the late twentieth century creates possibilities for decentralization and more equitable dispersion.

Itinerant healers are returning. They will ride the information superhighway.

Prisons /
Electronic Supervision Programs

Prisons, like hospitals, are places for involuntary, supervised confinement. Incarceration is supposed to take criminals out of circulation, punish them for their misdeeds, and perhaps reform them.

Medieval monasteries employed imprisonment in cells as a form of punishment; both Cluny and Hirsau had their windowless *carcer*.[36] And medieval castles were sometimes equipped with dungeons. When Carlo Fontana designed the San Michele prison for young men in Rome (which was to become the prototype for modern jails), he took the cell as his planning unit and provided rows of them on either side of a large central hall with altars at each end. Later prisons of the eighteenth and nineteenth centuries arranged cell blocks in radial or concentric patterns for ease of supervision

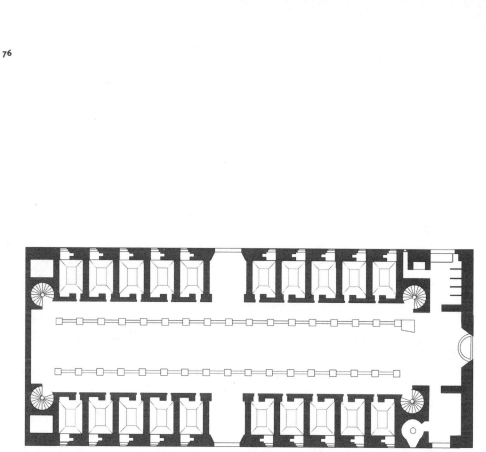

San Michele Prison, Rome, by Carlo Fontana (1703–4). Cells for the inmates surround a large, central workroom.

and control, or strung parallel blocks along lengthy circulation spines.

But electronics can now perform many of a prison's traditional functions without cells and walls — discipline and punishment *sans* slammer. Under the Electronic Supervision Program, some American offenders are sentenced to home detention and fitted with anklet transponders linked to telephone modems. A central monitoring station is automatically alerted whenever the wearer moves more than a specified distance from the modem — just as Fontana's unfortunate young detainees were confined to the vicinity of San Michele's altars.[37]

Elaborations of this strategy are easy to imagine and will be increasingly straightforward for enthusiastic law enforcement agencies to implement as wireless telecommunications technology evolves. Already, cops can have "drive-by" units to check on the location of offenders. Stores could have detectors for convicted shoplifters, playgrounds and schools could have them for pedophiles, and abused spouses could have them for their former partners. With more elaborate tracking technology, movements could be monitored continuously and cross-checked against crime scenes and times.

Of course the system would not be complete without effective ways to apply immobilizing force and punitive violence. But that doesn't seem too difficult. Anklets could automatically sound loud alarms when triggered by entry to forbidden places or when activated remotely by wardens. There might be some behavior-monitoring capacity built into an anklet or implant, together with a drug-release mechanism; one advocate of walking prisons imagines that "a sex offender's specific patterns of aberrant sexuality would be recognized by the programmed chip, and the drugs would selectively tone down criminally sanctioned behaviors but allow

normal or acceptable sexuality."[38] For maximum-security offenders, the drugs could be sleep-inducing or even lethal.

So the story that began with Carlo Fontana's schemes for San
Michele may be finally drawing to a close. The state will no longer
need walls and watchtowers to enact its legal monopoly on
confinement and violence. Telecommunications will do the job
instead.

BANKING CHAMBERS / ATMS

Asked why he robbed banks, the famous stickup artist (and jailbird)
Willie Sutton replied, "Because that's where the money is." But
postmodern thieves no longer break into vaults or terrorize tellers;
bent Baudrillardists, they have learned to bamboozle with floating
signifiers instead — because money, too, is now digital information
endlessly circulating in cyberspace.

In April 1993, at Buckland Hills Mall near Hartford, Connecticut,
some audacious PoMo-kleptos wheeled in a Fujitsu model 7020
automated teller machine — purportedly from a New Jersey bank
— and set it in operation.[39] When shoppers inserted their cards in
this con-robot, it electronically recorded the account and personal
identification number, then simply printed out slips saying that no
transactions were possible. Later, using counterfeit bank cards encoded with the pilfered numbers, the high-tech bandits began to
make cash withdrawals from ATMs in midtown Manhattan. What
was the scene of this scam? Where did the deed of milking the
moneypukers actually take place? Not, surely in Connecticut, New
Jersey, or New York, but somewhere deep in the cyberspace of
the ATM system.

This perplexing puzzle is one result of the wholesale shift of Main
Street banking to cyberspace that has taken place over the last

couple of decades. The first ATM machines was introduced by Citicorp in 1971; by 1980 there were fewer than twenty thousand ATM machines operating in the United States, but by 1990 there were more than eighty thousand. Today deposits and withdrawals only rarely take place at a traditional teller's window; by 1987 over 80 percent of bank customers used ATMs for more than half their transactions.[40]

When these devices were still new, and not yet well understood, they were sometimes treated as direct robotic replacements for human staff; you found them inside the bank, beside the counters where you filled out your deposit slips. But this missed the point; since ATMs depend on electronic rather than physical linkage to bank records, they do not really have to be inside under the eye of the manager. So they quickly migrated out onto the street, where they could operate twenty-four hours a day, seven days a week. Soon the realization dawned that they did not even have to stay attached to bank building facades; they could more effectively be located where crowds naturally congregated and where people actually *needed* cash — in supermarkets, shopping malls, airports, university student centers, and office building lobbies. Or, as in South Central Los Angeles or on the South Side of Chicago, they might more appropriately be placed in police station lobbies — where it was *safe* to collect cash. National and international ATM networks developed, so that you could get cash from machines that were far away from your hometown. The traditional Main Street bank building disintegrated, and the pieces that remained reintegrated themselves into new settings.

At the same time, electronic funds transfer networks have supplanted traditional heist bait — the stagecoach, the armored truck, and even (to some extent) the pocket full of cash. My paycheck is automatically, electronically transferred to my bank account each month, then some of it gets transferred out to make my mortgage

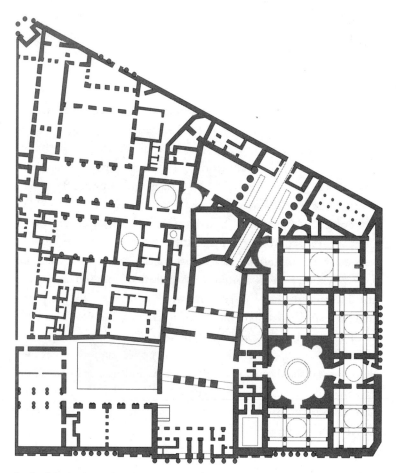

Bank of England, London, by John Soane (1788–1834). Each type of transaction has its own grand hall, and the various activities are connected through an intricate pedestrian circulation system.

payment. And CHIPS (the Clearing House Interbank Payments System, owned by a bunch of big New York banks) — just a couple of mainframe computers and a hundred or so dedicated phone lines in a nondescript Manhattan office building — processes trillions of dollars in payments, from banks all over the world, every day.[41] In 1980 daily electronic money transfers on CHIPS and the Fedwire network run by the Federal Reserve were about twelve times the balances held in accounts by the Federal Reserve; by 1990 the volume had grown to more than fifty times those balances. Money is no longer bullion in a strongbox, but bits in an online database.

By this point in the evolution of the digital era, we have almost forgotten the original *banchi* — the trestle tables at medieval fairs, where bankers and their clients met face-to-face to exchange promises.[42] Accommodating a bank's operations has ceased to be primarily a matter of providing appropriate rooms and circulation (as it was when Sir John Soane designed the Bank of England on three acres of ground in the heart of the City of London), but of configuring the right computer systems. Gaze in wonder at Soane's plan, noting the precisely differentiated functions of his great transaction halls — the Bank Stock Office, Accounts Office, Discount Office, even Five Pound Note Office; we will never see the like again. In sum, we are experiencing the step-by-step emergence of the soft bank — a round-the-clock facility, accessible from indefinitely many locations, and providing electronically mediated withdrawals, deposits, bill payments, check cashing, point-of-sale transactions, travelers' checks, loan applications, statements, and whatever other financial services the banking industry can dream up and sell.[43]

Even the now-ubiquitous ATMs (in their role as cash dispensers, at least) will become obsolete if coins and bills are eventually eliminated. This is a fairly straightforward technical possibility; a combination of network transfers, checks, credit cards, debit cards, ubiquitous point-of-sale terminals, and replacement of coin-operated gizmos like parking meters with electronic card-reading devices clearly could yield a cash-free society.[44] Personal terminals, for making and receiving payments anywhere, could be integrated with laptop or palmtop computers or could be specialized wallet-sized devices.

Not surprisingly, gambling casinos have led the way toward the cashless world. At Foxwood Casino, on the Mashantucket Pequot reservation in Connecticut, arriving customers obtain a "Wampum Card" — a smart debit card that electronically stores account balances and transaction records. The gaming tables are hooked into a computer network, and, brags the network's director, "We register a transaction every time the handle of a slot machine is pulled."[45]

Bank buildings, then, are no longer where the money is. They are shrinking to the point where they can no longer serve to celebrate financial institutions and transactions as Soane's great design so compellingly did. Indeed, cash money and associated transaction points may soon disappear entirely. Today's Willie Suttons are learning to crack computer security, not safes.

TRADING FLOORS / ELECTRONIC TRADING SYSTEMS

Historically, organized exchanges for common stock, futures, and option contracts have evolved as increasingly elaborate and specialized places for making deals. But they were simple in the beginning. The London Stock Exchange grew out of a coffeehouse where traders could meet. And in Vicenza on Tuesday mornings, in the old basilica that Palladio wrapped with his magical loggia, you can still see how modern commodity markets began: buyers

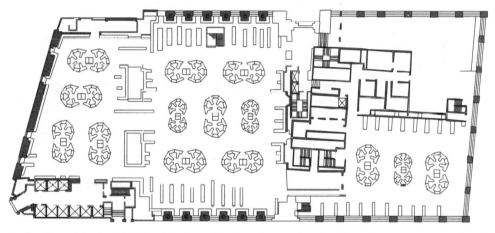

Trading floor of the New York Stock Exchange by George W. Post (1903) and Trowbridge & Livingston (1923). Trading posts for member firms are in the center, and telephone booths line the walls.

and sellers still transact their business in little wooden cubicles as they have for centuries.

When James Peacock designed a new building for the London Stock Exchange in 1801–2, European exchanges had evolved into voluntary associations of members who came together to trade securities in auction markets. A member would acquire the right to trade on the exchange by buying a "seat." The great exchanges of the nineteenth and twentieth centuries, like H. P. Berlage's monumental brick pile in Amsterdam, were organized around trading floors where the action took place. On Wall Street the floor of the New York Stock Exchange was planned with dumbbell-shaped "trading posts" for member firms in the center, telephone booths around the periphery, and plenty of room for pages to scurry back and forth with orders. The great boards flashed, the brokers shouted their bids and acceptances, and it was the very stuff of capitalist romance.

The telegraph and the telephone gradually began to change all that, of course. Geographically distributed over-the-counter (OTC) markets such as NASD (National Association of Securities Dealers) now bring together dealers who quote prices to buy and sell. They are not located on a trading floor somewhere; they might be anywhere. Seats become virtual.

The computer takes that process a big step further. By the early 1990s, trading floors everywhere were tumbling into obsolescence: the British and French stock markets had transformed into almost entirely computerized operations, the Toronto exchange was planning to shut down its floor, and the Korean and German exchanges were moving in the same direction.[46] Many stock transactions — perhaps the majority of them — had become computer-to-computer rather than person-to-person affairs. The US Treasury announced plans to introduce electronic bond auctions, in which

Wall Street dealers would submit bids electronically instead of phoning them in to government clerks, who scribbled them down.[47]

In 1992 Reuters, the Chicago Mercantile Exchange, and the Chicago Board of Trade opened Globex, a very ambitious twenty-four-hour electronic trading system for futures and options contracts. It took about as long to design and build (four years), and cost about as much ($70 million) as a major new trading building. But it has no floor; buy and sell orders are entered electronically into the system, prices are set by a process of computer matching with incoming orders, participants in the trade are properly notified, verification is sent to the Chicago exchange clearing center, and buyers' and sellers' accounts are adjusted — all in a few seconds. Its chairman claims, "This is a way to extend our market around the globe across all borders and time zones."

Globex has had its teething troubles, but it clearly shows us the financial future. Commentators on the financial markets (generally a pretty buttoned-down bunch) can now see a whole new world coming:

> The globalization of financial markets simultaneously fragments traditional financial transactions marketplaces and integrates them via electronic means. Physical marketplaces (the trading floors) are becoming obsolete, while "virtual" marketplaces — networks of computers and computer terminals — are emerging as the "site" for transactions. The new technology is diminishing the role for human participants in the market mechanism. Stock-exchange specialists are being displaced by the new systems, which by and large are designed to handle the demands of institutional investors, who increasingly dominate transactions. Futures and options floor traders also face having their jobs coded into computer algorithms,

which automatically match orders and clear trades or emulate open-outcry trading itself.[48]

This shift of financial markets to cyberspace has changed what is *being* traded. The 1990s saw the emergence on a huge scale of lightning-fast electronic trading in derivatives — sophisticated, computer-generated financial instruments that would be impossible without networks to move financial data around almost instantaneously and powerful workstations to perform the complex computations on which derivative transactions depend.[49] These pure creations of cyberspace — forwards, caps, collars, swaps, options, swaptions, and more — are essentially carefully calculated side bets on more traditional stock and bond investments. By 1994 the monthly volume of derivative trading on the New York Stock Exchange was running at twice the US gross domestic product.

Once, the canyon of Wall Street at the tip of Manhattan really was *the* place where stocks and bonds were traded — truly the capital of capital. Now (though the old thoroughfare remains and has become increasingly dense with electronics) it is the name of a flourishing region of cyberspace.

DEPARTMENT STORES / ELECTRONIC SHOPPING MALLS

Don't make the mistake of thinking that cyberspace marketplaces are all about mathematical whiz kids furiously trading esoteric derivatives, though. Even something as prosaic as the kitchen sink can now be offered and purchased electronically. When Matsushita opened a new-for-the-nineties kitchen showroom in Shinjuku, it was advertised as "the only place in the world where a person can walk in off the street and experience a high-tech Virtual Reality system in a consumer application."[50] You could strap on a headset and a data glove to inspect the appliances on offer. Actually, it didn't

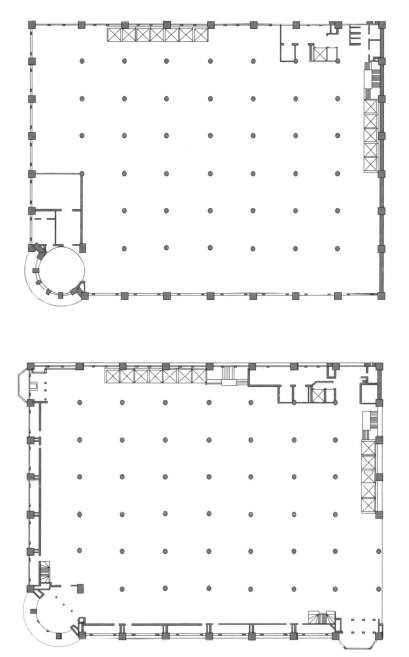

Carson, Pirie, Scott department store (formerly Schlesinger & Mayer), Chicago, by Louis H. Sullivan (1899–1904). Large, open floors linked by vertical circulation systems provide space for displays of goods.

work very well; the crude visual simulations approximated a condition of legal blindness, the gesture sensors recognized only a few simple hand and finger movements, and the heavy apparatus made your neck hurt. But by keeping the show and eliminating the room, it did save lots of very expensive Tokyo real estate.

It was only a transitional step. Once the traditional product showroom has been virtualized — replaced by a set of computer simulations — it can potentially be entered and explored from anywhere. (Elaborate virtual reality interfaces are probably unnecessary; on-command video clips of clothing being modeled, or viewer-controlled video cameras that can be used to inspect products remotely, can probably suffice to create effective virtual showrooms.) When there is enough network bandwidth, and when adequate display devices are sufficiently inexpensive and widespread, Shinjuku rents become irrelevant. The electronic mall becomes the digital successor to the Sears catalogue and the home shopping shows on cable television.

"Going shopping" now means something new.[51] Traditionally, it suggested a trip to market — contact with the historic urban center, a chance to mingle with fellow citizens. Market squares and market days were important spatial and temporal markers. The interface between stall or shop and public place was highly standardized; fronts were either left open to show the goods inside or (from the later seventeenth century) took the form of glazed display windows.[52] Groups of shops might be unified architecturally to yield grander urban elements, as in Giuseppe Mengoni's Milan Galleria. Alternatively, as the opening of the Bon Marché in Paris demonstrated in 1852, a multitude of departments might be combined in a single, great, vertically stacked store — a downtown place to which crowds of shoppers would swarm by train, tram, or bus.[53] More recently, these patterns have largely been displaced by the newer ones of driving to the suburban shopping mall or to the megawarehouse on the fringes of town.[54] But the electronic mall simply short-circuits the trip to a concentration of goods and displays, and replaces the glazed display window facing the street with windows on a computer screen.

Salesperson, customer, and product supplier no longer have to be brought together in the same spot; they just have to establish electronic contact. This idea was successfully pioneered in the phone-order computer business; the "stores" run by companies like Dell consist of toll-free telephone lines or computer network connections, warehouses located conveniently to transportation hubs, and United Parcel Service trucks equipped with wireless computers. A geographically distributed, electronically supported consumer transaction system completely replaces the traditional retail floor.

Even where familiar-looking retail stores remain, they are fast transmuting into computer-intensive network nodes. Bar code scanners at supermarket checkouts, terminals for credit card transactions, and wireless computers at rental car returns are the obvious first steps, but the close coupling of retail space to cyberspace can go far beyond that. Since the 1980s the retail chains Wal-Mart and Kmart have been using VSAT (Very Small Aperture Terminal) satellite systems to link widely scattered stores, delivery trucks, and warehouses into sophisticated computer systems for just-in-time inventory control, price updates, credit card authorization, and videoconferencing.[55] The same systems potentially allow on-shelf LED (light-emitting diode) displays of prices to be changed in all stores in a matter of seconds. Hand-held, wireless, inventory-tracking computers allow store assistants to check stock levels and prices and place orders without leaving the sales floor, and hand-held wireless sales terminals (much like electronic clipboards) are replacing fixed point-of-sale terminals in some stores.[56] Kmart's ShopperTrak system uses infrared sensors to track where the customers are in the store, to dispatch salespeople and open up checkout lanes when they are needed, and to provide information for setting advertising and display strategies.[57]

Increasingly though, merchants will find that they can dispense with sales floors and sales staff altogether and just maintain servers with databases of product specifications, prices, availability information, images, and simulations. The phone-order business becomes the network-order business. This arrangement potentially cuts overhead, taps into bigger markets, and lends itself to further automation at many levels. Product information can be adjusted instantly as supplies and prices change. Consumers might either "window shop" by remotely accessing such virtual stores, or they might delegate the task to software shopping agents that go out on the Net with shopping lists, inspect the specifications and prices of the merchandise on offer, and return with reports on the best available matches and prices. Closure of a sale can immediately trigger a delivery order at a warehouse, update an inventory database, and initiate an electronic money transfer. So, as the Internet has opened up to commercial use, as commercial online services have grown, and as switched video networks have emerged, schemes for cybershopping have proliferated. Consider some snapshots of pioneering entrepreneurial efforts, circa early 1990s.

Groceries. Plans announced for Time Warner's pilot Full Service Network in Orlando, Florida, include access to an interactive menu of 20,000 products from an online supermarket and 7,500 from a drugstore.[58] In these virtual stores, the act of shopping is scaled down to pointing and clicking; the shopper moves along "shelves" on which realistically rendered packages are displayed, drags items to a "cart," and eventually pays with a credit card. The order is then delivered at a prearranged time.

Automobiles. Contemplate Automall, another service announced for Time Warner's Orlando network. The idea is that viewers will interactively browse through selections of cars and trucks, configure the options, then ask a salesperson to bring a vehicle out to the house for a test drive.

Computers. At the bargain-basement, low-margin end of the computer business, the Internet Shopping Network went online in 1994 with a World Wide Web "storefront" and product catalogue accessed through Mosaic. When a customer selects a catalogue item, the system automatically verifies the customer's credit, scans the current inventory lists of suppliers, selects the lowest-cost combination of distributor, warehouse, and delivery service, and places the order. Delivery is by express package service. "When a customer pushes that button," the proprietor announced, "he's causing a product to be spit out the back of a warehouse with his name on it."[59]

Pizza.[60] Interactive television will replace the telephone. You enter a virtual pizza parlor and see a menu of available toppings. As you choose, a displayed pizza is modified accordingly and the price is tallied. When you are satisfied, the nearest pizzeria is notified and the order speeds to your door.

Clothing. Imagine a virtual clothing boutique. The catalogue is a large collection of video clips showing models wearing the items on offer; these clips can be accessed randomly from your home television set. (The president of Time Warner has commented: "We're talking about a fundamental shift in advertising. . . . You can bring the showroom to your house and take a 15-minute walk through it.")[61] Your detailed measurements are stored in a database somewhere. There is no inventory; when you place an order, computer-controlled machinery accesses these measurements and fabricates the item perfectly to your size. (Fitting rooms become unnecessary, and your size is never out of stock.) It is then delivered to your door.

With such soft shops, specialized retail districts and the departments that make up department stores simply become directory categories — logical groupings presented as menu items, icons, or virtual "storefronts" in the interfaces of online services. Retail location becomes a matter of being in the right directories. As with the old telephone Yellow Pages, customers let their fingers (or rather now, their cursors) do the walking. The stock is bigger and the selection larger than in the mightiest big-box off-ramp superstore. The things that remain in physical form are warehouses (which may become smaller as computerized inventory-control strategies become more sophisticated) and delivery vehicles.

From Kmart to Cybermart! Sic transit retail space?[62]

WORK / NET-WORK

Offices are sites of information work — specialized places where numbers, words, and sometimes pictures are collected, stored, transformed, and disseminated.[63] So their tissue is mostly composed of desks equipped with information-handling devices (telephones, computers, fax machines, printers, file cabinets, inboxes and outboxes, and the like), meeting and conference rooms, copying centers and mailrooms, and reception and circulation spaces.[64] From the economist's viewpoint, they are locations where value is added to information.

As information work has grown in volume and importance, and as increasingly efficient transportation and communication systems have allowed separation of offices from warehouses and factories, office buildings at high-priced central business district (CBD) locations have evolved into slick-skinned, air-conditioned, elevator-serviced towers. These architecturally represent the power and

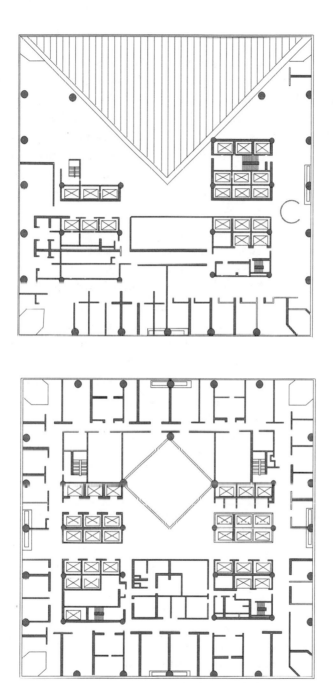

Typical floors of the Bank of China office tower, Hong Kong, by I. M. Pei and Partners (1990). Office workers are tightly packed into a slick-skinned, air-conditioned, elevator-serviced tower.

prestige of information-work organizations (banks, insurance companies, corporate headquarters of business and industrial organizations, government bureaucracies, law, accounting, and architectural firms, and so on) much as a grand, rusticated palazzo represented the importance of a great Roman, Florentine, or Sienese family. So, for example, when the Hong Kong and Shanghai Bank wanted to demonstrate its power and importance, it built a shiny high rise in the heart of Hong Kong's business district. Then the Bank of China trumped it by constructing a much taller tower on a nearby, overlooking site.

From this follows a familiar, widely replicated, larger urban pattern — one that you can see (with some local variants) from London to Chicago to Tokyo. The towers cluster densely at the most central, accessible locations in transportation networks. Office workers live in the lower-density suburban periphery and commute daily to and from their work. This tightly focused arrangement (as opposed to more diffuse distributions) allows considerable scale economies to be achieved in mass transit systems. Downtown services meet the needs of people in their worker roles during weekdays, while suburban services are there for those same people in their roles as residents in the evenings and on weekends.

The bonding agent that has held this whole intricate structure together (at every level, from that of the individual office cubicle to that of CBDs and commuter rail networks) is the need for face-to-face contact with coworkers and clients, for close proximity to expensive information-processing equipment, and for access to information held at the central location and available only there. But the development of inexpensive, widely distributed computational capacity and of pervasive, increasingly sophisticated telecommunications systems has greatly weakened the adhesive power of these former imperatives, so that chunks of the old structure have begun to break away and then to stick together again in new sorts of aggregations. We have seen the emergence of telecommuting, "the partial or total substitution of telecommunication, with or without the assistance of computers, for the twice-daily commute to/from work."[65]

Gobs of "back office" work can, for example, be excised from downtown towers and shifted to less expensive suburban or exurban locations, from which locally housed workers remain in close electronic contact with the now smaller but still central and visible head offices. These satellite offices may even be transferred to other towns or to offshore locations where labor is cheaper. (Next time you pay your credit card bill or order something from a mail-order catalogue, take a look at the mailing address. You'll find that the envelope doesn't go to a downtown location in a major city, but more likely to an obscure location in the heartland of the country.) The bedroom communities that have grown up around major urban centers also provide opportunities for establishing telecommuting centers — small, Main Street office complexes with telecommunications links to central offices of large corporations or government departments.[66] As a consequence, commuting patterns and service locations also begin to change; a worker might bicycle to a suburban satellite office cluster or telecommuting center, for example, rather than commute by car or public transportation to a downtown headquarters.

Another strategy is to create resort offices, where groups can retreat for a time to work on special projects requiring sustained concentration or higher intellectual productivity, yet retain electronic access to the information resources of the head office. This idea has interested Japanese corporations, and prototypes have been constructed at locations such as the Aso resort area near Kumamoto.[67]

In insurance companies, and other organizations that sell disembodied products or take orders to be filled later, traveling

salespeople can be readily transformed into high-technology nomads who remain continually online and almost never have to visit
the home office. For traditional centers of such industries, such as
Hartford, Connecticut, the future looks increasingly problematic as
the office-in-a-briefcase displaces the cubicle at corporate headquarters.[68]

More radically, much information work that was traditionally done
at city-center locations can potentially be shifted back to network-
connected, computer-equipped, suburban or even rural homes.
Way back in the 1960s, well before the birth of the personal
computer, James Martin and Adrian R. D. Norman could see this
coming. They suggested that "we may see a return to cottage
industry, with the spinning wheel replaced by the computer terminal" and that "in the future some companies may have almost
no offices."[69] The OPEC oil crisis of 1973 motivated some serious
study of the economics of home-based telecommuting.[70] Then the
strategy was heavily promoted by pop futurologists of the Reagan-
ite eighties, who argued that it would save workers the time and
cost of commuting while also saving employers the cost of space
and other overhead. The federal Clean Air Act amendments of
1990, which required many businesses with a hundred or more
employees to reduce the use of cars for commuting, provided
further impetus. More sober and skeptical commentators de-
murred, claiming that savings in commuting costs would be offset
and perhaps negated by the increased costs of distributing needed
supplies and utilities to workers at scattered locations, and that space
and overhead costs would not disappear but be transferred to the
workers. But by 1993 there was a clear and accelerating trend: there
were 6.6 million home-based telecommuters in the United States,
up 20 percent from 1991.[71]

At the same time, many observers have become convinced that the
very character of daily work is transforming in ways that reinforce

these tendencies. Robert Reich's policy tract *The Work of Nations* made a compelling case that advanced economies increasingly rely on highly skilled "symbolic processors" who deal mostly in information. Others have pointed out that, while information-work organizations once could accumulate and retain in fixed locations, over long terms, most of the expertise that they needed to carry on their businesses, this becomes increasingly difficult in an era of economic globalization and rapid political, social, and technological change. Now it is often better strategy to form multipartner, geographically distributed alliances of various specialist groups (consultants, suppliers, subcontractors, and so on) as needed for particular projects, then to disband and regroup as old projects end and new ones begin. We are entering the era of the temporary, recombinant, virtual organization — of business arrangements that demand good computing and telecommunications environments rather than large, permanent home offices.

In the 1960s and early 1970s, as the telecommunications revolution was rapidly gaining momentum, some urbanists leaped to the conclusion that downtowns would soon dissolve as these new arrangements took hold. Melvin Webber, for example, predicted: "For the first time in history, it might be possible to locate on a mountain top and to maintain intimate, real-time and realistic contact with business or other associates. All persons tapped into the global communications net would have ties approximating those used today in a given metropolitan region."[72]

There is some evidence that these theorists were right. Consider this telling straw in the electronic breeze. In 1974 Sears, Roebuck and Company proudly built Sears Tower in the Chicago Loop — 4.5 million square feet of floor space and the tallest building in the world, right in the birthplace of the office skyscraper. But Sears didn't stay there very long. By 1992 the company had deserted thirty-seven of the forty floors it occupied and sent five thousand jobs thirty-five miles west to Hoffman Estates in Chicago's suburban fringe.

But the prophets of urban dissolution underestimated the inertia of existing patterns, and the reality that has evolved in the 1980s and 1990s is certainly more complex than they imagined. The changing relative costs of telecommunication and transportation have indeed begun to affect the location of office work.[73] But weakening of the glue that once firmly held office downtowns together turns out to *permit* rather than *determine* dispersal; the workings of labor and capital markets and the effects of special local conditions often end up shaping the locational patterns that actually emerge from the shakeup.[74]

Perhaps the time has not yet come to bid farewell to those vertiginously vainglorious corporate monuments that have defined the great downtowns of the twentieth century. But they no longer seem so inevitable. Given a choice, many of us may prefer working with a net.

AT HOME / @HOME

The domestic living room is emerging as a major site at which digitally displaced activities are recombining and regrounding themselves in the physical world. It's not just in the homes of electroyuppies, digirati, and chiphead hobbyists. In many places now, news and entertainment, education, work, shopping and banking, and lots of general social interaction are starting to flow in and out through small, housebroken, electronic boxes. We are, it seems, seeing a reversal of the "gradual divorce of the home . . . from the workplace" that Lewis Mumford's narrative *The City in History* located in the seventeenth century.[75]

Couch potatoes and cable company executives have been quick to define the consumer electronic appliances that accomplish this as more intelligent descendents of the television set. But there is much more to them than that; they might equally well be regarded as smart, multimedia telephones or as domesticated computers.[76] They insinuate themselves in among familiar furnishings and appliances and displace or eliminate their roles.

In some ways, an information appliance hooked up to a high-bandwidth cable is a lot like an old-fashioned mailbox. It is where information streams into the house and is decoded, and, conversely, it is where information is encoded and sent out in digital form. But there is, of course, no need to hang it on the front door. It can be wherever cables can reach. It can even be wireless. The postman now knocks anywhere.

When attached to a display device (like a television set or personal computer monitor), such an appliance presents itself as a hearth that radiates information instead of heat. Just as the fireplace with its chimney and mantel was the focus of a traditional living room, and later became the pivot point for Frank Lloyd Wright's box-busting house plans, so the display — the source of data, news, and entertainment — now bids to become the most powerful organizer of domestic spaces and activities. In most rooms, it's what most eyeballs are most likely to lock onto most of the time.

Connected to an appropriate paper-processing mechanism, an appropriately configured information appliance can receive or send a fax, make a copy of a document, or deliver today's newspaper right into your hand. Printer, photocopier, fax machine, and newspaper delivery box all condense into one compact device. It becomes the new reading and writing desk, and it belongs in the study or the home office, beside the recycling bin.

An information appliance can also create electronic stoops — places where you can hear and be heard, or see (on a display) and be seen (via a video camera) without completely relinquishing the privacy and controllability of the home. But these places need not be positioned (like the old urban stoops lauded by nostalgic planning theorists) at the boundary between private property and the street; they can just as easily be internal, thus restructuring the traditional public-to-private hierarchies of domestic space.

For a designer of domestic space, these differences do matter. When information appliances are treated as interactive televisions or as electronic hearths, small groups of people will sit around them in living rooms, view them from distances of eight to ten feet, and probably control them with hand-held remote devices. Where they are assimilated to the tradition of the personal computer, individuals in dens and studies will view them from distances of about eighteen inches and use keyboards. If they are configured as two-way video-phones that create zones of semi-public space, then we will not want them in bedrooms or bathrooms, but if they are equipped with medical monitoring devices, then that is precisely where we will need them.

Increasingly, homes will be places with network addresses as well as street addresses. The functions of the various interior spaces will be established, in large part, through installation of specialized information spigots and collectors. And, as networks and information appliances deliver expanding ranges of services, there will be fewer occasions to go out.

DECOMPOSITION / RECOMBINATION

This sort of analysis reveals only part of the story, though. Efficient delivery of bits to domestic space will, in addition, collapse many of the spatial and temporal separations of activities that we have long taken for granted. Many of our everyday tasks and pastimes will cease to attach themselves to particular spots and slots set aside for their performance — workplaces and working hours, theaters and performance times, home and your own time — and will

henceforth be multiplexed and overlaid; we will find ourselves able
to switch rapidly from one activity to the other while remaining
in the same place, so we will end up using that same place in many
different ways. It will no longer be straightforward to distinguish
between work time and "free" time or between the space of production and the space of consumption. Ambiguous and contested
zones will surely emerge.

Imagine, for example, that you are in your living room at eight
o'clock in the evening. One window on your screen connects you
to a database on which you are paid to work, another shows the
news from CNN, and another puts you in a digital chat room. You
switch your attention back and forth — mostly dealing with the
database, but keeping an eye on the news and occasionally inter-
jecting a comment into the interesting conversation that is unfolding in the chat room. Children come and go, making their usual
demands, and you sometimes turn your attention to them. Are you
at work or at play? Should you be charging your time (or some
percentage of it) to your employer? If so, is your supervisor entitled
to check up on you by monitoring the screen display? Are you
occupying tax-deductible work space or nondeductible living
space?

Such instabilities and ambiguities in space use also challenge traditional ways of representing social distinctions and stages of sociali-
zation.[77] In many societies there are well-defined, separate places
in the dwelling for men, women, and children and for family
members and for guests; different information circulates in these
different spatial settings. Young children may be isolated and protected in nurseries and playgrounds, and there may be architecturally differentiated places for adolescents, adult breadwinners, and
retirees. At an urban scale, prisons, convents, residential colleges,
orphanages, hospices, halfway houses, official residences for political and religious leaders, and low-income housing projects make
vivid social distinctions by creating readily identifiable, physically

discrete domains. But categories lose their clarity, and rites of passage require redefinition, when the uses of built space are no longer permanently assigned and depend from minute to minute on software and the fleeting flow of bits.

Thus there will be profound ideological significance in the architectural recombinations that follow from electronic dissolution of traditional building types and of spatial and temporal patterns. Opposing ideologues have lost no time in pressing upon us their tendentious visions of this restructuring.

To the right, some futurologists (particularly Alvin Toffler)[78] have painted a neo-Norman Rockwell picture of cozy electronic cottages that "glue the family unit together again." As Toffler sees it, "The electronic cottage raises once more on a mass scale the possibility of husbands and wives, and perhaps even children, working together as a unit." With the anticipated decline in commuting to work, and the increasing possibility of changing jobs without changing houses, we can expect "greater community stability" and "a renaissance among voluntary organizations like churches, women's groups, lodges, clubs, athletic and youth organizations." He imagines a cozy return to the days of the loom in the living room, the farmhouse dairy, and merchants who lived above the shop, and to the community structures that accompanied these arrangements.

From the left, eliminating the spatial and legal distinctions between home and workplace usually looks more like an insidious strategy to decentralize and proliferate the Dark Satanic Mill. It removes the possibility of finding any refuge from the workplace, encourages long and irregular work hours, impedes organization of workers and regulation of workplace conditions, and puts women right back in the home. Domestic space becomes electronic sweatshop. In the resulting digital dystopia, "Landmarks are likely to be financial complexes and electronic skyscraper-fortresses, cordoned off from depleted and decaying inner city residential areas," while more affluent private estates and apartments are "sealed off from the surrounding community by elaborate surveillance and security systems."[79]

We can formulate these issues in social equity terms. Shall we allow home-based employment, education, entertainment, and other opportunities and services to be channeled to some households and not to others, thereby technologically creating and maintaining a new kind of privilege? Or can we use the infobahn as an equalization mechanism — a device for providing enhanced access to these benefits for the geographically isolated, the homebound elderly, the sick and disabled, and those who cannot afford wheels?

We can also formulate them as questions about architecture's fundamental representational role. If we can no longer make the traditional urban distinction between, on the one hand, major public and commercial buildings that represent institutions, and, on the other hand, relatively uniform and repetitive housing areas, how shall we make social organization and power legible? Going out, going to work, going to school or to church, going away to college, and going home are economically significant, socially and legally defining, symbolically freighted acts. To change or eliminate them, as electrocottages and cybercondos promise to do, is to alter the basic fabric of our lives.

PROGRAMMABLE PLACES

Building type by building type, the story is much the same. The floor plan of a traditional store, library, theater, school, bank, stock exchange, office, home, or any other kind of building clearly shows how it works: you see particular places for the various activities that are to be housed, together with a circulation system of doors and passageways that integrates these parts into a functioning whole. If you look at the site plan, you can also see how entry and exit points, windows, and walls relate the whole composition to its natural setting or urban context. And at an urban scale, streets and public places interconnect buildings. Classical architects of the eighteenth and nineteenth centuries handled the task of putting spaces together by creating hierarchies of great and small spaces around axial, symmetrical circulation systems connected to grand, formal entries and public open spaces.[80] With the aim of being as logical and efficient as possible, functionalist modernists of the twentieth century have often derived their less regular layouts directly from empirically established requirements of adjacency and proximity among the necessary spatial elements.[81]

But when telecommunication through lickety-split bits on the infobahn supplements or replaces movement of bodies along circulation paths, and when telepresence substitutes for face-to-face contact among the participants in activities, the spatial linkages that we have come to expect are loosened. The constituent elements of hitherto tightly packaged architectural and urban compositions can begin to float free from one another, and they can potentially relocate and recombine according to new logics. Perhaps it is not too romantic to imagine that unique natural environments, culturally resonant urban settings, and local communities that hold special social meaning will increasingly reassert their power. Perhaps we will find compelling advantages to putting together spaces — like living spaces and work space — that were once thought to belong in different buildings located in different zones of the city. In any case, the old bonds break down and new groupings can begin to form.

Simultaneously, the fresh requirements of the infobahn age suddenly kick in. Buildings and parts of buildings must now be related not only to their natural and urban contexts, but also to their cyberspace settings. Increasingly, they must function as network interfaces — loading docks for bits. They must be equipped with electronic sensors and effectors, onboard processing power, sophisticated internal telecommunications capabilities, software, and capacity for getting bits on and off — much like computer screen space that can be programmed for many different uses. Instead of living rooms, we will have domestic spaces that can be programmed for work, education, and entertainment. In place of today's centralized schools and hospitals, we will have systems for projecting specialized expertise into many different places — from airplane seats to isolated rural community centers — wherever and whenever it is required. Instead of building huge suburban theme parks filled with different rides, entertainment moguls will construct networks of much smaller, reprogrammable, simulation rides.[82] Rooms and buildings will henceforth be seen as sites where bits meet the body — where digital information is translated into visual, auditory, tactile, or otherwise perceptible form, and, conversely, where bodily actions are sensed and converted into digital information.

Building these programmable places is not just a matter of putting wires in the walls and electronic boxes in rooms (though that is a start). As the relevant technologies continue to develop, miniaturized, distributed computational devices will disappear into the woodwork. Keyboards and mouse pads will cease to be the only bit-collection zones; sensors will be everywhere. Displays and effectors will multiply. In the end, buildings will become computer interfaces and computer interfaces will become buildings.

Architects of the twenty-first century will still shape, arrange, and connect spaces (both real and virtual) to satisfy human needs. They will still care about the qualities of visual and ambient environments. They will still seek commodity, firmness, and delight. But commodity will be as much a matter of software functions and interface design as it is of floor plans and construction materials. Firmness will entail not only the physical integrity of structural systems, but also the logical integrity of computer systems. And delight? Delight will have unimagined new dimensions.

5

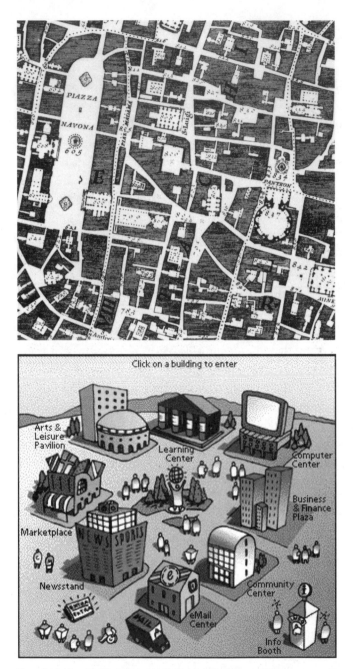

Two city maps: Nolli's Rome and Apple's e•World.

In a world of ubiquitous computation and telecommunication, electronically augmented bodies, postinfobahn architecture, and big-time bit business, the very idea of a city is challenged and must eventually be reconceived. Computer networks become as fundamental to urban life as street systems. Memory and screen space become valuable, sought-after sorts of real estate. Much of the economic, social, political, and cultural action shifts into cyberspace. As a result, familiar urban design issues are up for radical reformulation.

REAL ESTATE / CYBERSPACE

I was there at the almost-unnoticed Big Bang — the silent blast of bits that begat the new communities of the digital era. It was UCLA, fall 1969, and I was a very young assistant professor writing primitive CAD software and trying to imagine the role that designers might play in the emerging electronic future. In a back room just down the hallway from the monster mainframe on which I worked, some Bolt Beranek and Newman engineers installed a considerably smaller machine that booted up to become the very first node of ARPANET — the computer network that was destined to evolve into the worldwide Internet.[1]

From this inconspicuous point of origin, network tentacles grew like kudzu to blanket the globe. By December there were four

ARPANET nodes. In April 1971 there were 23, in June 1974 there were 62, and in March 1977 there were 111. Soon, cyberspace was busting out all over: two more important networks, CSnet (funded by the National Science Foundation) and BITNET (funded by IBM) developed in the early 1980s. A high-speed backbone (NSFnet) was in place by July 1988; this connected thirteen regional networks scattered across the United States — much as the interstate highway system linked local road networks — and the whole loosely organized system became known as the Internet. During the late 1980s and early 1990s more and more networks connected to the Internet, and by 1993 it included nearly two million host computers in more than 130 countries. In the first six months of 1994 more than a million additional machines were hooked up.

In the United States, by that point, there was one Internet host for every couple of hundred people.[2] (Take care in interpreting these figures, though; the actual density is likely to be much higher in affluent, computer-literate places like Cambridge, Massachusetts, and Palo Alto, California, and much lower in inner-city Detroit or East Los Angeles.) According to the best estimates — but in truth, nobody really knew — there were more than thirty million active users.[3]

While the Internet community was evolving into something analogous to a ramshackle Roman Empire of the entire computer world, numerous smaller, independent colonies and confederations were also developing. Dial-in bulletin board systems such as the Sausalito-based WELL — much like independent city-states — appeared in many locations to link home computers.[4] Commercial online services such as Compuserve, Prodigy, and America Online emerged in parallel to the government-sponsored, education- and research-oriented Internet. Before long, though, most of these erstwhile rivals found it necessary to join forces with the Internet.

There would not have been a great deal to connect if computers had remained as large and expensive as they were when AR-PANET began in 1969. But as networks developed, so did inexpensive personal computers and mass-marketed software to run on them. The very first, the Altair, showed up in 1974, and it was followed in the early 1980s by the first IBM PCs and Apple Macintoshes. Each one that rolled off the assembly line had its complement of RAM and a disk drive, and it expanded the potential domain of cyberspace by a few more megabytes of memory.

Somewhere along the line, our conception of what a computer *is* began to change fundamentally. It turns out that these electronic boxes are not just big, fast, centralized calculating and data-sorting machines, as ENIAC, UNIVAC, and their mainframe successors had led us to believe. No, they are primarily *communication* devices — not dumb ones like telephone handsets, that merely encode and decode electronic information, but smart ones that can organize, interpret, filter, and present vast amounts of information. Their real role is to construct cyberspace — a new kind of place for human interactions and transactions.

WILD WEST / ELECTRONIC FRONTIER

The early days of cyberspace were like those of the western frontier. Parallel, breakneck development of the Internet and of consumer computing devices and software quickly created an astonishing new condition; a vast, hitherto-unimagined territory began to open up for exploration. Early computers had been like isolated mountain valleys ruled by programmer-kings; the archaic digital world was a far-flung range in which narrow, unreliable trails provided only tenuous connections among the multitudinous tiny realms. An occasional floppy disk or tape would migrate from one to the other, bringing the makings of colonies and perhaps a few unnoticed viruses. But networking fundamentally changed things — as clipper ships and railroads changed the preindustrial world — by linking the increasingly numerous individual fragments of cyberturf into one huge, expanding system.

By the 1990s the digital electronics and telecommunications industries had configured themselves into an immense machine for the ongoing production of cyberspace. We found ourselves rapidly approaching a condition in which every last bit of computer memory in the world would be electronically linked to every other. And those links will last forever. Because its electronic underpinnings are so modular, geographically dispersed, and redundant, cyberspace is essentially indestructible. You can't demolish it by cutting links with backhoes or sending commandos to blow up electronic installations, and you can't even nuke it. (The original ARPANET was, in fact, explicitly designed to withstand nuclear attack.) If big chunks of the network were to be wiped out, messages would automatically reroute themselves around the damaged parts. If some memory or processing power were to be lost, it could quickly be replaced. Since copies of digital data are absolutely exact replicas of the originals, it doesn't matter if the originals get lost or destroyed. And since multiple copies of files and programs can be stored at widely scattered locations, eliminating them all with certainty is as hard as lopping Hydra heads.

Cyberspace is still tough territory to travel, though, and we are just beginning to glimpse what it may hold. "In its present condition," Mitch Kapor and John Perry Barlow noted in 1990, "cyberspace is a frontier region, populated by the few hardy technologists who can tolerate the austerity of its savage computer interfaces, incompatible communications protocols, proprietary barricades, cultural and legal ambiguities, and general lack of useful maps or metaphors." And they warned, "Certainly, the old concepts of property, expression, identity, movement, and context, based as they are on physical manifestation, do not apply succinctly in a world where there can be none."[5]

This vast grid is the new land beyond the horizon, the place that beckons the colonists, cowboys, con artists, and would-be conquerors of the twenty-first century. And there are those who would be King.

H U M A N   L A W S   /   C O D E D   C O N D I T I O N A L S

Out there on the electronic frontier, code is the law. The rules governing any computer-constructed microworld — of a video game, your personal computer desktop, a word processor window, an automated teller machine, or a chat room on the network — are precisely and rigorously defined in the text of the program that constructs it on your screen. Just as Aristotle, in *Politics,* contemplated alternative constitutions for city-states (those proposed by the theorists Plato, Phaleas, and Hippodamos, and the actual Lacedaemonian, Cretan, and Carthaginian ones), so denizens of the digital world should pay the closest of critical attention to programmed polity. Is it just and humane? Does it protect our privacy, our property, and our freedoms? Does it constrain us unnecessarily or does it allow us to act as we may wish?

At a technical level, it's all a matter of the software's conditionals — those coded rules that specify *if* some condition holds, *then* some action follows. Consider, for example, the familiar ritual of withdrawing some cash from an ATM. The software running the machine has some gatekeeper conditionals; *if* you have an account and *if* you enter the correct PIN number (the one that matches up, in a database somewhere, with the information magnetically encoded on your ATM card), *then* you can enter the virtual bank. (Otherwise you are stopped at the door. You may have your card confiscated as well.) Next the program presents you with a menu of possible actions — just as a more traditional bank building might present you with an array of appropriately labeled teller windows or (on a larger scale) a directory pointing you to different rooms: *if* you indicate that you want to make a withdrawal, *then* it asks you to specify the amount; *if* you want to check your balance, *then* it prints out a slip with the amount; *if* you want to make a deposit, *then* yet another sequence of actions is initiated. Finally, the program applies a banker's rule; *if* the balance of your account is sufficient (determined by checking a database), *then* it physically dispenses the cash and appropriately debits the account.

To enter the space constructed by the ATM system's software you have to submit to a potentially humiliating public examination — worse than being given the once-over by some snotty and immovable receptionist. You are either embraced by the system (if you have the right credentials) or excluded and marginalized by it right there in the street. You cannot argue with it. You cannot ask it to exercise discretion. You cannot plead with it, cajole it, or bribe it. The field of possible interactions is totally delimited by the formally stated rules.

So control of code is power. For citizens of cyberspace, computer code — arcane text in highly formalized language, typically accessible to only a few privileged high-priests — is the medium in which intentions are enacted and designs are realized, and it is becoming a crucial focus of political contest. Who shall write the software that increasingly structures our daily lives? What shall that software allow and proscribe? Who shall be privileged by it and who marginalized? How shall the writers of the rules be answerable?

F A C E - T O - F A C E / I N T E R F A C E

The most basic built-in rules of virtual places control when you can act, what kinds of actions you can take, and who or what you can affect by your actions. Old computer graphics hackers, for example, fondly remember *Spacewar,* the first computer game; it provided a diagrammatically depicted, deep-space battlefield in which players could take turns moving simulated spaceships, launching missiles, and amiably attempting to blow each other to bits.[6] On timesharing systems, players did not have to share a single console but could operate individually from their own. And when networks began to develop, so did remote *Spacewar* between players who might be hundreds of miles apart. But the game stayed the same. The relationships that mattered were not those of the players' bodies in physical space (as, for example, in a pistol duel) but those of their surrogates in cyberspace, and the rules that counted were the coded-in ones of the virtual place in which the surrogates met.

On the early bulletin boards and commercial networks, "forums" or "rooms" that allowed participants to "chat" quickly became a main attraction.[7] Here the rules structured not a shoot-'em-up arena but a space for (mostly) risk-free, multiparticipant conversation. The place that you entered was presented as a scrolling text window. It had a descriptive or evocative name (like a bar, coffee shop, or other such hangout), and you could survey the scene by looking at a list of current participants. At any point, you could type in a short text comment; this appeared in the window, preceded by your chosen online handle, so that a stream of comments scrolled by on each participant's screen — a geographically distributed, highly stylized, cocktail party with electronically masked participants and a mouse in your hand instead of a drink.

Forum habitués would often bar crawl from room to room until they found one that seemed to have the right buzz. If they struck up an interesting conversation, they could agree to go off into private rooms to continue, and eventually might even contemplate the big step of choosing times and physical locations to go face-to-face with new-found friends.[8] So these virtual places performed, in a vivid new way, the traditional urban function of creating opportunities for chance encounters between strangers. And the associated conventions allowed those encounters to evolve, step by step, toward friendship and intimacy. Not surprisingly, some of these convivial spots became hot hangouts in cyberspace.

In the early days of computer networks it seemed a slightly far-fetched metaphor to describe these sorts of interaction sites as "places," since bandwidth was narrow and communication was mostly restricted to typing and receiving text. But SIMNET changed that.[9] A military project dating from the interregnum when ARPA was DARPA, SIMNET first came online in 1986 as a network of M-1 tank simulators, and it has since been elaborated to include other types of vehicles. The viewports of the "tanks" are video screens displaying simulated three-dimensional terrain over which a mock tank battle takes place. Since the computer-generated display is updated in real time as controls are manipulated, dozens of widely scattered tank crews have the vivid impression of maneuvering around the same patch of countryside. Perhaps fittingly, this prototypical electronic landscape — this Garden of Eden of cyberspace — is a realistically simulated battlefield.

The technology of distributed interactive simulation (DIS) systems grew out of SIMNET, and by the early 1990s it was being hyped as the latest thing for the theme park industry.[10] Pretty soon you could line up to play *BattleTech, Virtuality,* or *Fightertown* — interactive games unfolding in networked simulator pods that immerse you in tacky but fairly convincing virtual worlds.

As bandwidth burgeons and computing muscle continues to grow, cyberspace places will present themselves in increasingly multisensory and engaging ways.[11] They will look, sound, and feel more realistic, they will enable richer self-representations of their users, they will respond to user actions in real time and in complex ways, and they will be increasingly elaborate and artfully designed. We will not just look *at* them; we will feel present *in* them.[12] We can expect them to evolve into the elements of cyberspace construction — constituents of a new architecture without tectonics and a new urbanism freed from the constraints of physical space.

ON THE SPOT / ON THE NET

Why do some places attract people? Often, it is because being on the spot puts you in the know. The merchants' coffeehouses of eighteenth-century New York, for instance, provided opportunities to get the latest shipping information, to meet potential trading partners, and to exchange other important commercial information.[13] Depending on your trade, you might find the need to locate in the financial district, the garment district, or SoHo, on Harley Street, Fleet Street, or Lincoln's Inn Fields, in Hollywood, Silicon Valley, or Detroit. You might be attracted to the literary salon, the corner saloon, or the Cambridge high table. It's not just a matter of where the jobs are, but of where you can exchange the most up-to-date, specialized information with the most savvy people; you may be able to do the same work and pursue similar interests if you are out in the sticks, but you are likely to feel cut off and far from the center of things.

In cyberspace, list servers soon evolved to perform some of the same functions. These are programs for broadcasting e-mail messages to all the "subscribers" on specified address lists. They are like electronic Hyde Park Corners — places in which anybody can stand up and speak to the assembled crowd. Lists may assemble formal groups such as the employees of a business, or the students enrolled in a class, or they may be constructed through some informal, self-selection process. As with physical assemblies, some lists are public and some secret, some are open to anybody and some are rigorously exclusive.

Electronic "newsgroups" were also quick to develop. Newsgroup software allows participants to "post" text messages (and sometimes other sorts of files), much as you might pin printed notices to a physical bulletin board. The notices — queries, requests, responses, news items, announcements, tips, warnings, bits of gossip, jokes, or whatever — stay there until they are deleted, and anyone who enters the place can read them. Usually there is a host — a sort of Cyber de Staël or Virtual Gertrude presiding over an online rue de Fleury — who sets topics, coaxes the exchanges along when they flag, and occasionally kicks out an unruly or objectionable partici-pant.[14] By the 1990s there were countless thousands of these places, advertising every interest you might imagine and some that you surely would not. If you wanted to be in touch and up with the latest in your field, it was increasingly important to have ready access to the right newsgroups. And your physical location no longer mattered so much.

When there is a sudden need, ad-hoc newsgroups can spring almost instantly into existence. Within hours of the January 1994 Los Angeles earthquake, there was a Usenet newsgroup called *alt.current-events.la.quake*. Long before the rubble had been swept from Wilshire Boulevard and before telephone service had unjammed, it was providing a place to post damage reports and find news about friends and relatives. It was the best place to be if you wanted to know what was going on.

The virtual communities that networks bring together are often defined by common interests rather than by common location: Unix hackers, Amiga enthusiasts, Trekkies, and Deadheads are scattered everywhere. But the opposite can also be true. When networks and servers are organized to deal with information and issues of local concern to the people of a town or to the students, staff, and faculty of a university, they act to maintain more tradi-tional, site-specific communities. So, for example, the City of Santa

Monica's pioneering Public Electronic Network (PEN) is available only to residents of Santa Monica, to people who work in the city, or at thirty-five public-access terminals located within the city boundaries.[15] And the Athena educational network was put in place on MIT's Cambridge campus to serve the MIT community.

STREET NETWORKS / WORLD WIDE WEB

Ever since Ur, urban places have been linked by movement channels of various kinds: doorways and passageways have joined together the rooms of buildings, street grids have connected buildings to each other, and road and rail networks have allowed communication between distant cities. These familiar sorts of physical connections have provided access to the places where people lived, worked, worshipped, and entertained themselves.

Now there is a powerful alternative. Ever since the winter of 1994, I have had a remarkable piece of software called Mosaic on the modest desktop machine that I'm using to write this paragraph.[16] (Right now, Mosaic is open in another window.) Mosaic is a "client" program that provides convenient access to World Wide Web (WWW) servers located throughout the Internet. These servers present "pages" of information, which may be in the form of text, graphics, video, or sound. Pages typically have "hyperlinks" pointing to related pages elsewhere in the Web, allowing me to jump from page to page by clicking on highlighted text or images.

The "home page" of any WWW server invites me to step, like Alice through the looking glass, into the vast information flea market of the Web — a cyberspace zone now consisting of countless millions of interconnected pages. The astonishing thing is that a WWW page displayed on my screen may originate from a machine located *anywhere* on the Internet. In fact, as I move from page to page, I am logging into computers scattered around the world.

But as I see it, I jump almost instantaneously from virtual place to virtual place by following the hyperlinks that programmers have established — much as I might trace a path from station to station through the London Underground. If I were to diagram these connections, I would have a kind of subway map of cyberspace.

Neighborhoods / MUDs

MUD crawling is another way to go. Software constructions known as MUDs, Multi-User Dungeons, have burned up countless thousands of log-in hours since the early 1980s.[17] These provide settings — often very large and elaborately detailed ones — for online, interactive, role-playing games, and they often attract vast numbers of participants scattered all over the Internet. They are cyberspace equivalents of urban neighborhoods.

The particular joy of MUDville is the striking way that it foregrounds issues of personal identity and self-representation; as newcomers learn at old MUDders' knees, your first task as a MUD initiate is to construct an online persona for yourself by choosing a name and writing a description that others will see when they encounter you.[18] It's like dressing up for a masked ball, and the irresistible thing is that you can experiment freely with shifts, slippages, and reversals in social and sexual roles and even try on entirely fantastic guises. You can discover how it *really* feels to be a *complete* unknown.

Once you have created your MUD character, you can enter a virtual place populated with other characters and objects. This place has exits — hyperlinks connecting it to other such settings, which have in turn their own exits. Some heavily frequented MUDs are almost incomprehensibly vast, allowing you to wander among thousands of distinct settings, all with their own special characteristics, like Baudelaire strolling through the buzzing complexity of nineteenth-century Paris. You can examine the settings and objects that you encounter, and you can interact with the characters that you meet.

But as you quickly discover, the most interesting and provocative thing about a MUD is its constitution — the programmed-in rules specifying the sorts of interactions that can take place and shaping the culture that evolves. Many are based on popular fantasy narratives such as *Star Trek,* Frank Herbert's *Dune,* C. S. Lewis's *Chronicles of Narnia,* the Japanese animated television series *Speed Racer,* and even more doubtful products of the literary imagination; these are communities held together, as in many traditional societies, by shared myths. Some are set up as hack-'n-slash combat games in which bad MUDders will try to "kill" your character; these, of course, are violent, Darwinian places in which you have to be aggressive and constantly on your guard. Others, like many of the TinyMUDs, stress ideals of constructive social interaction, egalitarianism, and nonviolence — MUDderhood and apple pie. Yet others are organized like high-minded lyceums, with places for serious discussion of different scientific and technical topics. The MIT-based *Cyberion City* encourages young hackers — MUDders of invention — to write MUSE code that adds new settings to the environment and creates new characters and objects. And some are populated by out-of-control, crazy MUDders who will try to engage your character in TinySex — the one-handed keyboard equivalent of phone sex.

Early MUDs — much like text-based adventure video games such as *Zork* — relied entirely on typed descriptions of characters, objects, scenes, and actions. (James Joyce surely would have been impressed; city as text and text as city. Every journey constructs a narrative.) But greater bandwidth, faster computers, and fancier programming can shift them into pictorial and spatial formats.[19] Lucasfilm's *Habitat,* for example, was an early example of a graphic

MUD that had its first incarnation, in North America, on the QuantumLink Club Caribe network (a precursor of America Online) and Commodore 64 computers. Later, it spawned a colony, *Populopolis,* that reputedly attracted a lot more paying customers on the NIFtyServe network in Japan.[20]

As a citizen of *Habitat,* you could customize your character, known as your Avatar, by selecting from a menu of body parts and choosing a sex.[21] (That was a one-bit choice, since *Habitat* was marketed as fairly conservative family entertainment.) Players conversed with one another in comic strip speech balloons. A region — one of as many as 20,000 similar ones in the original *Habitat* at its zenith — was a place that you can walk your character around, and it had doors and passages to other regions. These regions were filled with functional objects such as ATM machines to provide cash, bags and boxes to carry things in, books and newspapers to read, weapons, flashlights, and garbage cans. You could walk, take elevators, or teleport to other regions and explore them; you could exchange conversation, buy and sell goods, and even swap body parts. And, if you got tired of your character, you could reconfigure it, give it some drugs, or take it to the Change-o-matic sex-change machine.

As the creators of *Habitat* soon found, their task became one of reinventing architecture and urban design for cyberspace. They commented:

> For 20,000 Avatars we needed 20,000 "houses" organized into towns and cities with associated traffic arteries and shopping and recreational areas. We needed wilderness areas between the towns so that everyone would not be jammed together into the same place. Most of all, we needed things for 20,000 people to do. They needed interesting places to visit — and since they can't all be in the same place at the same time, they needed a *lot* of interesting places to visit —

and things to do in those places. Each of those houses, towns, roads, shops, forests, theaters, arenas, and other places is a distinct entity that someone needs to design and create.[22]

Only limitations in bandwidth and processing power inhibit taking the next step — the realization of whizzier World Wide Webs, superMUDs, and other multiparticipant, urban-scale structures consisting of hyperlinked, three-dimensional, sensorily immersive spaces. And these limitations are temporary. The online environments of the future will increasingly resemble traditional cities in their variety of distinct places, in the extent and complexity of the "street networks" and "transportation systems" linking these places, in their capacity to engage our senses, and in their social and cultural richness.

But no matter how extensive a virtual environment or how it is presented, it has an underlying structure of places where you meet people and find things and links connecting those places. This is the organizing framework from which all else grows. In cyberspace, the hyperplan is the generator.

ENCLOSURE / ENCRYPTION

You don't get to go just *anywhere* in a city, and the same is true of cyberspace. In both domains, barriers and thresholds play crucial roles.

In the built fabric of a city, the enclosing surfaces of the constituent spaces — walls, floors, ceilings, and roofs — provide not only shelter, but also privacy. Breaches in these surfaces — gates, doors, and windows — incorporate mechanisms to control access and maintain privacy; you can lock your doors or leave them open, lower the window shades or raise them. Spatial divisions and access-control devices are carefully deployed to organize places into hierarchies grading from completely public to utterly private. Sometimes you have to flip your ID to a bouncer, take off your shoes, pay admission, dress to a doorman's taste, slip a bribe, submit to a search, speak into a microphone and wait for the buzzer, smile at a receptionist, placate a watchdog, or act out some other ritual to cross a threshold into a more private space. Traditions and laws recognize these hierarchies and generally take a dim view of illicit boundary crossing by trespassers, intruders, and Peeping Toms.

Different societies have distinguished between public and private domains (and the activities appropriate to them) in differing ways, and urban form has reflected those distinctions. According to Lewis Mumford, domestic privacy was "a luxury of the well-to-do" up until the seventeenth century in the West.[23] The rich were the people who could do pretty much what they wanted, as long as they didn't do it in the street and frighten the horses. As privacy rights trickled down to the less advantaged classes, the modern "private house" emerged, acquired increasingly rigorous protections of constitutional law and public policy, and eventually became the cellular unit of suburban tissue.[24] Within the modern Western house itself — in contrast to some of its ancient and medieval predecessors — there is a staged gradation from relatively public verandahs, entry halls, living rooms, and parlors to more private, enclosed bedrooms and bathrooms, where you can shut and lock the doors and draw down the shades against the outside world.

It doesn't rain in cyberspace, so shelter is not an architectural issue. But privacy certainly is. So the construction technology for virtual cities — just like that of bricks-and-mortar ones — must provide for putting up boundaries and erecting access controls, and it must allow cyberspace architects and urban designers to organize virtual places into public-to-private hierarchies.

Fortunately, some of the necessary technology does exist. Most obviously, in cyberspace construction the rough equivalent of a locked gate or door is an authentication system.[25] This controls access to virtual places (such as your e-mail inbox) by asking for identification and a password from those who request entry. If you give the correct password, you're in.[26] The trouble, of course, is that passwords, like keys, can be stolen and copied. And they can sometimes be guessed, systematically enumerated until one that works is found, or somehow extorted from the system manager who knows them all. So password protection — like putting a lock on a door — discourages illicit entry but does not block the most determined break-in artists.

Just as you can put the valuables that you *really* want to protect in a sturdy vault or crypt, though, you can build the strongest of enclosures around digital information by encrypting it — scrambling it in a complex way so that it can be decoded only by someone with the correct secret numerical key. The trick is not only to have a code that is difficult to crack, but also to manage keys so that they don't fall into the wrong hands. The cleverest known way to do this is to use a technique called RSA public-key encryption. In this system, which derives its power from the fundamental properties of large prime numbers, each user has both a secret "private" key and a "public" key that can be distributed freely. If you want to send a secure message, you obtain the intended recipient's public key and use it to encode the information. Then the recipient decodes the message using the private key.

Under pressure from cops and cold warriors, who anticipate being thwarted by impregnable fortresses in cyberspace, the US federal government has doggedly tried to restrict the availability of strong encryption software. But in June 1991, hacker folk hero Philip Zimmerman released his soon-to-be-famous, RSA-based Pretty Good Privacy (PGP) encryption program. By May 1994 commercial versions had been licensed to over four million users, and MIT had released a free, noncommercial version that anybody could legally download from the Internet.[27] From that moment, you could securely fence off your private turf in cyberspace.

Meanwhile, the Clinton administration pushed its plans for the Clipper Chip, a device that would accomplish much the same thing as RSA but would provide a built-in "trapdoor" for law-enforcement wiretapping and file decoding.[28] The effect is a lot like that of leaving a spare set of your front door keys in a safe at FBI headquarters. Opinion about this divided along predictable lines. A spokesman for the Electronic Frontier Foundation protested, "The idea that the Government holds the keys to all our locks, before anyone has even been accused of committing a crime, doesn't parse with the public."[29] But an FBI agent, interviewed by *The New York Times,* disagreed: "O.K., someone kidnaps one of your kids and they are holding this kid in this fortress up in the Bronx. Now, we have probable cause that your child is inside this fortress. We have a search warrant. But for some reason, we cannot get in there. They made it out of some new metal, or something, right? Nothing'll cut it, right? And there are guys in there *laughing* at us. That's what the basis of this issue really is — we've got a situation now where a technology has become so sophisticated that the whole notion of a legal process is at stake here. . . . If we don't want that, then we have to look at Clipper."[30]

So the technological *means* to create private places in cyberspace are available, but the *right* to create these places remains a fiercely contested issue. Can you always keep your bits to yourself? Is your home page your castle?[31] These are still open questions.

PUBLIC SPACE / PUBLIC ACCESS

Once public and private spaces are distinguished from each other they can begin to play complementary roles in urban life; a well-organized city needs both.[32] And so it is in cyberspace. At the very least, this means that some part of our emerging electronic habitat should be set aside for public uses — just as city planners have traditionally designated land for public squares, parks, and civic institutions. Public pressure for this grew in the 1990s as the importance of cyberspace became increasingly clear. In 1994, for example, Senator Inouye of Hawaii introduced to the US Senate a bill that would reserve 20 percent of all new telecommunication capacity for free, public uses (noncommercial educational and informational services and civic discourse) and would provide funding for those uses.[33]

But urban public space is not merely un-private — what's left over when everyone walls off their private domains. A space is genuinely public, as Kevin Lynch once pointed out, only to the extent that it really is openly accessible and welcoming to members of the community that it serves.[34] It must also allow users considerable freedom of assembly and action. And there must be some kind of public control of its use and its transformation over time. The same goes for public cyberspace, so creators and maintainers of public, semipublic, and pseudopublic parts of the online world — like the makers of city squares, public parks, office building lobbies, shopping mall atriums, and Disneyland Main Streets — must consider who gets in and who gets excluded, what can and cannot be done there, whose norms are enforced, and who exerts control. These questions, like the complementary ones of privacy and encryption, have become the foci of crucial policy debates.

The Internet and commercial online services like America Online and Compuserve have to date provided only semipublic cyberspace at best, since they are widely but not universally accessible; you have to belong to a subscribing organization or have to pay to get in. This begs the question of how truly public cyberspace — the equivalent, say, of the Piazza San Marco in Venice — might be constructed. The community networks that emerged in the 1980s and 1990s — Santa Monica Public Electronic Network, Blacksburg Electronic Village, Telluride InfoZone, Smart Valley, and Cambridge Civic Network, for example — sought answers by trying to make network access openly available to entire communities in the same way that city hall and the local public parks traditionally have been.[35]

Many of these community networks are structured as so-called free-nets, in which a "city" metaphor is explicitly used to structure information access: you go to the appropriate "building" to find the information or services that you want. Thus the "welcome" screen of the Cleveland Free-Net (one of the oldest and largest, with more than 35,000 registered users and over 10,000 log-ins per day) presents the following quotidian directory:

1. The Administration Building
2. The Post Office
3. Public Square
4. The Courthouse and Government Center
5. The Arts Building
6. Science and Technology Center
7. The Medical Arts Building
8. The Schoolhouse (Academy One)
9. The Community Center and Recreation Area
10. The Business and Industrial Park
11. The Library
12. University Circle
13. The Teleport
14. The Communications Center
15. NPTN / USA Today Headline News

On the free-net model, then, the new, virtual city becomes a kind of electronic shadow of the existing physical one. In many (though not all) cases, a citizen can choose between going to an actual public building or to the corresponding virtual one.

But a free-net's superimposition of the virtual onto the physical, while sensible enough, is not a logical or technical necessity. In fact, one of the most interesting questions for twenty-first-century urban designers to ask is, "How *should* virtual and physical public space relate to one another?"

Consider the obvious options. There is complete dissociation of the two if the electronic public space is accessible only from personal computers in homes and businesses. Another possibility is to associate access points with civic architecture: put an electronic information kiosk in the lobby of city hall or in the public library, for example. The Berkeley Community Memory and Santa Monica PEN systems have demonstrated a more radical strategy by placing rugged workstations in places like laundromats and at congregation points for the homeless; these workstations thus begin to play a public role much like the traditional one of fountains in the public places of Rome. The artist Krzysztof Wodiczko has gone a step further by suggesting that the physically homeless and displaced might carry electronic "alien staffs" — personal devices that connect them to cyberspace and sometimes construct public representations of self by providing information to others about who they are and where they come from. These are public rather than personal digital assistants.

Since physical distance means little in cyberspace, the possibility also exists to "condense" scattered rural communities by creating public spaces that serve large, thinly populated areas. The Big Sky Telegraph, which has been running in Montana since 1988, successfully pioneered this idea.[36] It began by linking one-room and two-room rural schoolhouses across the state, and it has focused on education, economic opportunity, and economic self-sufficiency. In economically disadvantaged communities, where adequate public facilities of a traditional kind do not exist, the possibility of providing public cyberspace may become an important community development issue. Increasingly, communities and their planners will have to consider tradeoffs between investing scarce resources in creating or upgrading parks and community buildings and putting the money into effective electronic networks.

Whatever approach is taken to deploying network capacity for public purposes, though, simply making computers available and providing some kind of electronic access to civic information and discourse is not enough to create successful public cyberspace. Just as parks and squares must be pleasant and welcoming to a diverse population in order to function effectively, so must the interfaces to public areas of cyberspace; an interface that depends on cryptic commands and arcane knowledge of computer technology is as much a barrier to most people as is a flight of steps to a park user in a wheelchair. People must also feel secure and comfortable — not subject to hostility, abuse, or attack. And more subtly, but just as importantly, the cultural presumptions and cues that are built into an interface must not discourage potential users.[37] Think of important physical public spaces like New York's Central Park and consider the extent to which both their successes and their failures depend on these sorts of things; designers of public cyberspace will have to deal with them as well.

COMMUNITY CUSTOMS / NETWORK NORMS

Where public cyberspace exists, how can and should it be used? Do the customs and laws that govern physical public space still make sense in this new context?

As usage of the Internet and commercial online services has grown, there have been increasingly frequent disputes that have tested the limits of acceptable behavior in electronic public places and raised the question of how these limits might reasonably be enforced. In April 1994, for example, some particularly thick-skinned lawyers from Phoenix spammed the Internet by indiscriminately spraying a commercial advertisement for the services of their firm into thousands of newsgroups.[38] This blast of unwanted bits had the same effect as driving a blaring sound truck into a public park. The Internet community reacted with outrage and disdain, and flamed back tens of thousands of complaints. One of the unrepentant perpetrators proclaimed his right to be a pain and threatened to do it again. Eventually — to cries of "censorship!" from some quarters — a young Norwegian programmer wrote and unleashed an effective piece of "cancelbot" software that sniffed out and automatically removed the offending advertisements wherever they showed up.[39]

In another widely publicized incident that unfolded almost simultaneously, a graduate student at MIT was busted by the FBI for operating an Internet bulletin board that had become a very active site for illegal activity — much like a bar in which drug deals were going down. Copies of commercial software were being posted, then downloaded without payment by users who logged in from all over the world. Was the operator of this openly accessible place responsible for knowing and controlling what was going on there? Or could he rightfully claim that it was just none of his business?

Like the proprietors of shopping malls and Disneylands, the operators of commercial online services must struggle with the inherently contradictory nature of the semipublic places they create. On the one hand, these places need lots of paying customers to support them, so they have to seem as welcoming, open, and inclusive as possible. On the other hand, though, the operators want to stay in firm control of what goes on. (The question is often framed as one of whether these services should be regarded as common carriers, like the telephone companies, and therefore not responsible for any libelous, obscene, or criminal information that they might carry or whether they should be in control and therefore held responsible like book and newspaper publishers and television broadcasters.) The last time I peeked at Prodigy, for example, I found the following notice from the management (a bit like the "Do not spit" signs that used to appear in railway stations): "And please remember that PRODIGY is for people of all ages and backgrounds. Notes containing obscene, profane or sexually explicit language (including descriptions of sexual acts, and whether or not masked with 'x's and the like) are not allowed. A good test is whether the language in your note would be acceptable at a public meeting."

Prodigy explicitly aims at a family audience, so it remorselessly enforces the norms of Middle America.[40] Its competitors Compuserve and Genie have different sorts of constituencies, but their operators also take care to remove messages they consider obscene or illegal. And America Online has shut down some feminist discussion forums because, according to a spokesperson, kids might see the word "girl" in the forum's headline and "go in there looking for information about their Barbies."[41] The excluded feminists might be forgiven for responding in not-for-prime-time language. And forget the 'x's. These places have found a useful role to play, but don't mistake them for genuine, open-to-all, watch-out-for-yourself spaces for unconstrained public discourse.

Some institutions are even more restrictive. My daughter's high school treats its corner of public cyberspace as a schoolyard where teachers enforce discipline. When the kids first got e-mail addresses, they were asked to sign contracts banning "sexually explicit speech." Then, when the inevitable happened, and some students complained about receiving obscene messages, the e-mail system was temporarily shut down as punishment.

But then, there will always be a Berkeley! The Berkeley Community Memory system is a radical political invention — a transposition of the Free Speech Movement and People's Park into cyberspace.[42] All information on the system is community generated, postings can be anonymous, and no central authority controls the content of postings. Funding is decentralized as well: there are coin-operated terminals on which postings can be read without charge, but it costs a quarter to post an opinion and a dollar to open up a new forum.

NOLLI AND THE NET

The story of virtual communities, so far, is that of urban history replayed in fast forward — but with computer resource use playing the part of land use, and network navigation systems standing in for streets and transportation systems. The WELL, the World Wide Web, MUDs, and Free Nets are — like Hippodamos's gridded layout for Miletos, Baron Haussmann's radial patterning of Paris, or Daniel Burnham's grand plan for Chicago — large-scale structures of places and connections organized to meet the needs of their inhabitants.

And the parallels don't stop there. As traditional cities have evolved, so have customs, norms, and laws governing rights to privacy, access to public and semipublic places, what can be done where, and exertion of control. The organization of built space into public-to-private hierarchies, with gates and doors to control boundary crossings, has reflected this. Nolli's famous map of Rome vividly depicted it. Now, as cyberspace cities emerge, a similar framework of distinctions and expectations is — with much argument — being constructed, and electronic plazas, forums, lobbies, walls, doors, locks, members-only clubs, and private rooms are being invented and deployed. Perhaps some electronic cartographer of the future will produce an appropriately nuanced Nolli map of the Net.

6

Electronically mediated transactions: Krzysztof Wodiczko, "Alien Staff" and "Porte-Parole."

Follow the money! If you want to understand how a community — physical or virtual — has grown and survived, look to its economic base.

You will see that the ancient cities of Mesopotamia, the Nile, the Indus, and the Yellow River were made possible by invention of the wheel, the plow, and the irrigation ditch; they emerged in the midst of fertile agricultural hinterlands and busied themselves with the accumulation and exchange of excess agricultural production. When barbarian invaders threatened, cities like Rome and Constantinople became fortified enclosures with large military populations engaged in protecting the citizenry and civil institutions. With

the development of maritime trade, Venice, Pisa, and Genoa — owing to their favorable locations — flourished as mercantile centers. With steam and steel in the nineteenth century came mushrooming industrial cities like Manchester and Pittsburgh. And in the soft cities of cyberspace the economic engine is the bit business — the production, transformation, distribution, and consumption of digital information.[1]

ECONOMICS 101 / ECONOMICS 0 AND 1

Colin Clark's textbook-enshrined distinctions among economic sectors suggest that we should expect, first of all, to find a primary production level at the foundation of the bit business. And indeed, useful information is now continually harvested from the world by keyboards, microphones, video cameras, surveillance satellites, point-of-sale terminals, and desktop document scanners, and then stored in databases like wheat in silos. There are innumerable small operations, and there are a few massive bit extraction and refining enterprises, such as those converting large libraries and image collections into digital form and putting them online.

At the level corresponding to secondary industry in Clark's schema, raw bits are transformed into information products and distributed to consumers. Here, software takes command; its role in information economies is similar to that of industrial machinery and manufacturing plants in industrial ones. (Some day, perhaps, some enterprising urban historian will produce a history of industrial and commercial application software that parallels Sigfried Giedion's cataloguing and celebration of early machines in *Mechanization Takes Command*.) Sometimes production and distribution operations are related in something approximating the traditional, industrial way — as when a publisher uses databases and document-production software to create a newsletter, then e-mails copies to subscribers. Increasingly, though, the production capabilities are shifting to the consumer end — as when a wire service feed flows into a personal computer, where stories are automatically selected and laid out by personal newspaper-production software. Potentially, each node in a computer network is both a production and a consumption site for information products, and the channels carry a complex, multiway information trade.

In cyberspace, the tertiary Clarkian level becomes that of information retailers, brokers, agents, and middlemen. The editors and publishers of a scientific journal, for example, provide the essential services of evaluating the relevance and scientific merit of submitted papers and selecting the best for publication. Though production and distribution mechanisms for traditional print journals and emerging online journals are very different, this information-brokering function remains. Similarly, when gatherings shift from bars to bulletin boards, there is still a need for somebody to serve as "innkeeper" to keep the premises in order and the conversation moving along. And as retailing and banking go online, sales jobs move to cyberspace.

Networks and cyberspace communities connect players in the different sectors, much as transportation systems and cities on the ground have always done. Like farmers putting their wheat on the railroad to get it to markets and consumers, primary producers of information can put their bits on the Net. Manufacturers of information products can find suppliers and raw materials on the Net, then ship their finished work back out. Sales people and professional consultants can set up shop at network addresses instead of at locations on Main Street. If you surf around the World Wide Web for a while, or explore the offerings of any commercial online service, you will find booming activity at all of these levels.

TANGIBLE GOODS / INTELLECTUAL PROPERTY

This activity only exists, of course, because people have come to value bits. So they are willing to spend resources on creating, acquiring, storing, transforming, and transferring bits. They find that they are interested in trading bits, and in many cases they want to protect their bits.

Lawyers like to look at valuable bits as a form of intellectual property, like texts printed on paper or movies distributed on videotape. They reason that incentives for the creation of digital works are needed, so creators should have limited monopolies that allow them to make money from their intellectual contributions while society as a whole benefits from the production and distribution of knowledge. It follows, then, that cyberspace economic activity should be regulated by copyright and patent law, though perhaps modified and extended to take account of the novel characteristics of digital media and distribution systems.

But the "property" metaphor can be misleading, since digital artifacts (such as application software files, text files, and digital movies and audio files) differ from tangible property like land, buildings, automobiles, and printed books in several crucial ways.[2] They can be reproduced indefinitely at trivial cost, and through telecommunications networks they can be distributed almost instantaneously throughout the world. They take up very little storage space, and they can often be moved around undetectably. In many contexts, it is quick and easy to transform and combine existing digital information to produce new works that may seem very different.

Most importantly perhaps, one person's use of a file or some application software need not interfere with or prevent another's use of the same resource. Land is different: if I build on a lot, then you cannot. So are automobiles: if I have the family car, then you do not. So, even, are books and videotapes: if I check out a copy of some work from the library, then other users cannot. By contrast, the digital resources that are available in cyberspace do not *have* to be scarce resources. And it is a queer kind of property that can be valuable without being intrinsically scarce.

Because of these differences, the growing cyberspace business community is finding that it cannot rely on either the traditional legal mechanisms for protecting the bits that it sells and barters or on familiar ways of assuring payment. Infobahn-oriented strategies are emerging. For example, providers of news archives and other large, frequently updated databases may charge users not for the information that they download but for the time spent logged in to the provider's server to conduct searches; since the retrieved information is most valuable when it has been extracted from the latest version of the database, users have an incentive to perform (and pay for) new searches rather than to rely on bootleg copies of the results of old searches. Or, where users receive continuous streams of information — as in the case of the news feeds that are used to create personalized newspapers — payment can be by subscription; where subscriptions are not paid, the information stream can be cut off. In the case of online books and journals, and of movies on demand, providers can maintain comprehensive online catalogues that allow users to get quickly and conveniently to what they want, then the providers can charge fees for downloading the material to the user's printer or viewing device.

Invention of mechanisms like these is one part of the answer to the problem of constructing a workable framework for cyberspace business — one that adequately protects the originators and distributors of bits, while avoiding unnecessary impediments to the free flow of information. Another part is the development of intellectual property law to cover the new situations that arise in cyberspace. Yet another — perhaps most important of all — is the emergence of a broadly shared sense of morality in these matters. Whatever technical and legal controls are implemented will succeed only to the extent that they have community acceptance; unresolved moral disputes will create conflict among members of cyberspace communities just as surely as they do in other contexts.

Moving Material / Processing Bits

It would be easy to miss the point by pushing this sort of analysis to its logical extreme and so concluding that cyberspace economic activity operates autonomously in its own realm — disconnected from material, place-based operations. But bits often have value precisely because they tell us something about the material world and can usefully guide our actions in that world. In fact, the electronic linkages of cyberspace largely serve (as Manuel Castells has put it) to "connect agriculture and manufacturing with the consumption of goods and services, and with the management of organizations and institutions of society."[3] The emerging result seems to be a complex interaction between established, geographically located urban and regional economies and the increasingly powerful effects of long-distance, almost instantaneous information flows within worldwide virtual communities.

Geographers, economists, and planners will have to gather data and do some careful analysis to sort out what is really going on, but here are some plausible guesses. First, there are growing forces acting to *decentralize* economic activity. Managers and professionals are increasingly able to scatter across the globe while reintegrating their activities through telecommunications. The mobility of capital has been heightened. A world economy can now function in real time. Firms can maintain unity of management while decentralizing production and participating in markets worldwide. At the same time, there are some vigorous *centralizing* forces. Production processes remain ultimately dependent on appropriation and transformation of matter, so industrial locations are still largely determined by local availability of raw materials and access to labor markets. Furthermore, the initial development of an advanced telecommunications infrastructure is likely to favor existing urban centers (with their high and profitable concentrations of information work) over small towns and remote areas. In the end, these opposing forces will have complex and socially differentiated effects on urban and regional development processes and on industrial, commercial, and residential locational patterns. There is no simple formula.

So cyberspace communities — like eighteenth-century seaports, nineteenth-century railroad towns, and mid-twentieth-century motel/fast-food strips — play specialized roles within the complex new economic order that develops as a new kind of infrastructure

is deployed. They are stops on the infobahn. The world's apparently
insatiable greed for bits will fuel their growth, as demand for
manufactured goods drove development of earlier industrial cities
and transportation centers. They will flourish as places to make
bucks from bits by producing them, owning them, moving them,
brokering them, gambling with them, skimming them, stealing
them, and inventing new ways to add value to them.

PHYSICAL TRANSACTIONS / ELECTRONIC EXCHANGES

Historically, communities have fostered economic activity by providing specialized settings for buyers and sellers to meet and exchange goods and services.[4] In *Politics* Aristotle proposed that a city
should have both a "free" square in which "no mechanic or farmer
or anyone else like that may be admitted unless summoned by the
authorities" and a marketplace "where buying and selling are done
. . . in a separate place, conveniently situated for all goods sent up
from the sea and brought in from the country."[5] Ancient Rome
had both its *fora civilia* for civic assembly and its *fora venalia* for the
sale of food. These Roman markets were further specialized by type
of produce; the *holitorium* was for vegetables, the *boarium* for cattle,
the *suarium* for pigs, and the *vinarium* for wine. Medieval marketplaces were places both for barter and exchange and for religious
ritual. Modern cities have main streets, commercial districts, and
shopping malls jammed with carefully differentiated retail stores in
which the essential transaction takes place at the counter — the
point of sale — where money and goods are physically exchanged.

In cyberspace the necessary connection of buyers and sellers is
established not through physical proximity but through logical
linkage. It is all done with software and databases. Merchants get
to potential customers by accessing lists of electronic addresses; the
key to successful marketing is not being in the right neighborhood

with the right sorts of customers for whom to lay out wares, but (as with the older strategy of direct-mail marketing) having the right lists for sending out advertising. Conversely, customers get to merchants by accessing online catalogues; to search efficiently for particular goods, they need appropriate collections of catalogue pointers rather than convenient access to specialty stores and shopping districts. Lists of lists and catalogues of catalogues provide convenient starting points for making business connections, much as merchants of different kinds might cluster together in a bazaar or shopping center.[6]

Technically, then, the logical pointers linking merchants and customers can run in either direction. But there is a question of who is in control. Do the merchants compile, maintain, sort, and filter all the databases, and decide when and where to direct their advertising? This raises questions about possible invasion of privacy by pinpoint marketers, of how customers can fend off unwanted advertising, of who has the right to initiate transactions, and of whether some groups may be systematically denied information about things that they need (a new form of redlining).[7] Or do customers construct and maintain databases of pointers to catalogues they find useful and get product information only when they request it? This makes it difficult to market new products and difficult for new merchants to break into markets. So a successful cyberspace marketplace probably needs some appropriate balance of the two.

The Prodigy online service, initiated by Sears and IBM in the 1980s, was a pioneering attempt to construct a cyberspace consumer marketplace. Prodigy was designed from the outset to carry advertising and to create records of which advertisements had been viewed. Users were also asked to provide demographic information. This information was then used to "personalize" content. The service agreement defined the arrangement clearly: "One of the valuable and unique features of the Prodigy service is its ability to personalize information and transaction services to each Member's interests. Personalization is based on data provided by the Member (or Membership Holder) to Prodigy, data derived from the Member's use of the Prodigy service, and from the Member's responses to Prodigy's questions and surveys."[8]

In this and other cyberspace consumer marketplaces, the merchants have so far had all the advantages. They have been the ones with the big computers and the capacity to put together lists by recording credit card, telephone, and home computer transactions and buying mailing lists.[9] But we can expect this balance to shift as more and more customers have computers and network connections, and as client software like Mosaic and Netscape makes it easier for them to find and search catalogues. As the necessary technology evolves, we may find that an increasing amount of business is done by the highly personalized software agents of customers (who know the habits and preferences of their masters) meeting the sales agents of merchants in virtual showrooms and stores.

Immaterial goods such as insurance policies and commodity futures are most easily traded electronically. The idea is readily extended to small, easily transported, high-value specialty items — books, computer equipment, jewelry, and so on — the sorts of things that have traditionally been sold by mail order. But it makes less sense for grocery retailing and other businesses characterized by mass markets, high bulk, and low margins. Cyberspace cities, like their physical counterparts, have their particular advantages and disadvantages for traders, so they are likely to grow up around particular trade specializations.

BANK NOTES / ELECTRONIC CASH

Since you cannot literally lay down your cash, sign a check, produce a credit card, or flash an ID in cyberspace, payment methods are being reinvented for this new kind of marketplace. The Internet and similar networks were not initially designed to support commercial transactions nor secure enough for this purpose. Fortunately, data encryption techniques can be used to authenticate the identities of trading partners, to allow secure exchange of sensitive information such as credit card numbers and bid amounts, and to affix digital "signatures" and time stamps to legally binding documents. By the summer of 1994, industry standards for assuring security of Internet transactions were under development, and online shopping services were beginning to offer encryption-protected credit card payment.[10]

But credit card payment — no matter how secure and fraud-resistant it can be made — has the disadvantage that it does not provide the anonymity of cash payment; whenever a credit card is used for a purchase, the vendor can keep a record of the number. Furthermore, cross-linking of credit card records can be used to generate detailed purchasing, travel, communication, and medical histories of individuals. So various "electronic cash" schemes have been developed to provide security for network financial transactions while maintaining the privacy of principals.

Electronic cash schemes typically make use of digital signatures in some way; a secret key is used to "sign" messages, then a public key is used to verify them, and *only* a message signed by the private key can be verified by the public key.[11] Thus a bank might issue "electronic bank notes" in the form of numbered bundles of bits signed with a particular private key. Different denominations would have different private keys. To withdraw a dollar from the bank, you would send a message with your private key, and the bank would debit your account and send back an electronic bank note signed with its private key. To spend that dollar, you would send it back to the bank, which would verify the signature, check the number against the list of notes already spent, then transfer a dollar to the payee's account.[12]

While this straightforward approach provides good security, it does not allow anonymous payments; the bank can still keep a record of who spent which notes and where they were spent. So more elaborate schemes, such as that developed by the DigiCash company, provide for "blinding" notes by employing mathematical tricks with random numbers.[13]

Though the underlying mechanics of electronic cash may seem complicated, the user interface need not be. Online, users could simply drag icons representing bank notes to graphically depicted payment locations. On the street, users could carry their electronic cash in electronic wallets.

Whatever forms of electronic payment eventually gain wide acceptance, they promise fundamental changes in our daily lives. In traditional cities the transaction of daily business was accomplished literally by handing things over; goods and cash crossed store counters, contracts were physically signed, and perpetrators of illegal transactions were sometimes caught in the act. But in virtual cities, transactions reduce to exchanges of bits.

HELOTS / AGENTS

Transactions in cyberspace, like those that take place in more traditional settings, are not always conducted directly by the principals. Sometimes it's a case of "My assistant will call your assistant": the task is delegated to agents. Use of agents frees your time for other things, which becomes particularly important when the transactions that you must conduct are numerous and time-consuming.

As online activity has grown, so has the realization that the denizens of cyberspace, like the Greek citizens contemplated in Aristotle's *Politics,* will need the help of reliable agents to do their bidding. Aristotle, notoriously, described the kind of agents that he had in mind — human slaves — as "live tools" needed to support the "good life." He elaborated: "Tools may be animate as well as inanimate; for instance, a ship's captain uses a lifeless rudder, but a living man for watch; for a servant is, from the point of view of his craft, categorized as one of its tools. So any piece of property can be regarded as a tool enabling a man to live, and his property is an assemblage of such tools; a slave is a sort of living piece of property." Then he went on to imagine, as an aside, a species of artificially intelligent tools that would bail him out of the mess that this morally obtuse line of reasoning had landed him in: "For suppose that every tool we had could perform its task, either at our bidding or itself perceiving the need, and if — like the statues made by Daedalus or the tripods of Hephaestus . . . — shuttles in a loom could fly to and fro and a plucker play a lyre of their own accord, then master craftsmen would have no need of servants nor masters of slaves."[14]

Such automata were not available in ancient Greece, but in cyberspace they are; programmers can construct intelligent bit puppets — software tools to do their bidding. The idea of autonomous software agents that can not only perform useful tasks, but also — at least to some extent — learn from experience and make certain decisions on their own goes back to some investigations in the 1960s by the artificial intelligence pioneer Oliver Selfridge.[15] In the 1980s Marvin Minsky's book *The Society of Mind* provided inspiration and some important technical underpinnings.[16]

By the 1990s the vast scale of the online world and the huge bit glut that it provided had made agents seem a necessity. They began to show up in some MUDs, where software objects known as bots may interact with human players to serve as guides, to hawk real estate, and sometimes even to sucker the unwary into TinySex. Serious users of online information began to rely on search agents that know where to find certain sorts of material, can go out on the network and get it for you, and can perhaps even present it in convenient and attractive formats of your own choosing.[17] Desperate users of e-mail began to employ agents that would filter out junk mail and prioritize the rest. Newsgroup junkies turned with relief to the Stanford Netnews Filter, which reads all 10,000-plus newsgroups on the Usenet message network each day and e-mails back the ones containing specified key phrases. Engineers created agents to control electricity networks, and astronomers used agents to schedule telescope time.[18] Personal computers began to lodge agents that would watch users transacting their daily business of answering correspondence and scheduling meetings, look for patterns, and automate these where appropriate.[19] And as more and more business is transacted in cyberspace, it seem inevitable that we will see increasing use of agents that automatically seek out offers of goods and services, negotiate prices, and make purchases. Let your agents do the walking!

Early in 1994 the general public began to hear a lot more about the hitherto esoteric topic of agents when General Magic — a much watched and talked-about Silicon Valley startup — rolled out its *Telescript* and *Magic Cap* software. *Telescript* is a specialized programming language for conveniently creating agents and virtual places. *Magic Cap* is an entry point to this world of agents and places — a graphic operating system that presents cyberspace as a cute, Disneyland-like "Main Street" filled with "shops" maintained by organizations that want to hawk their wares and services. You can go shopping yourself, by entering programmed places and interacting with the agents that you find there. Or you can delegate the task by sending your agents out to meet other agents.

As software agents have appeared on the scene, more and more cyberspace places have acquired attendants that guide you through whatever is available there and help you to make use of it — much as shops have shop assistants, offices have receptionists, hotels have concierges, and libraries have librarians. In MUDs — in a new twist on the Turing test — visitors sometimes find it difficult to tell whether they are interacting online with fellow humans or with clever pieces of software.

It isn't hard to imagine the social and urban problems that could emerge as agent populations grow.[20] Computer viruses and worms are maliciously constructed agents — fanning out, like Fagin's boys, to cause trouble. Will there will be a criminal underclass? Will faulty programming produce destructive, uncontrollable rogue agents? Since agents are easy to reproduce, cyberspace may be flooded with billions of them; how will population be controlled? How will the law deal with agents that perform important tasks on behalf of distant, perhaps oblivious originators?[21] Even if our agents turn out to be very smart, and always perform impeccably, will we ever fully trust them? And how will we deal with the old paradox of the slave? We will want our agents to be as smart as possible in order to do our bidding most effectively, but the more intelligent they are, the more we will have to worry about losing control and the agents taking over.

So history replays itself. The great cities of the past required large labor forces to run them; they imported slaves or attracted immigrants seeking work. So Greek and Roman houses had slave quarters, slums grew up in the shadows of factories in nineteenth-century industrial cities, and modernist architects of the early twentieth century became preoccupied with providing inexpensive, high-density (often high-rise), repetitive worker housing. And the burgeoning, increasingly indispensable, programmed proletariats of cyberspace cities now live invisibly on disk drives.

JURISDICTIONS / LOGICAL LIMITS

Within any community, some kinds of transactions are sanctioned and others, like selling drugs, may not be. So the significance of city boundaries has traditionally been that they marked the limits of a community's power to establish and enforce controls on what inhabitants could do: inside the walls, a community's norms and laws applied, but outside they did not. Plutarch vividly expressed the importance of the boundary by telling how Romulus plowed a deep furrow to delineate the periphery of Rome and thought the task so important that he killed the interfering Remus. Roman law provided severe punishment for those who tampered with boundary stones, and the Roman pantheon gave a proud place to Terminus, god of boundaries.

Today, the maps negotiated by politicians and drafted by urban planners are patchworks of ownership boundaries, zoning boundaries, and jurisdictional boundaries. Within jurisdictional borders, local laws and customs apply, local power is exerted by some over others, and local police and military forces maintain power by the potential or actual use of violence. But bits answer to terminals, not Terminus; these lines on the ground mean little in cyberspace.

Consider, for example, control of images that have been defined by those in authority as pornographic. There was a time when governments could effectively control the images by policing production and distribution within their boundaries and confiscating publications at the border. (Some mullahs and isolationist despots still get away with it.) But it is very difficult — sometimes impossible — to create effective border checkpoints in cyberspace. Now, digital images and videos can be posted on bulletin boards that are physically located anywhere in the world and downloaded by anyone, anywhere, who has a network connection.[22] If they are downloaded through the Internet, the multiplicity of possible transmission paths, and the use of a packet-switching protocol — which means that files are sent in fragments to be reassembled at the receiving end — makes transmissions particularly difficult to intercept.

In 1994 the proprietors of an "adult" image server called Amateur Action Bulletin Board, which was physically located in Milpitas,

California, were hauled into federal court in Memphis, Tennessee, and convicted on a charge of distributing pornography.[23] The action followed a raid on the bulletin board premises by US postal agents and San Jose police officers. The prosecution claimed that image files downloaded from the bulletin board violated local Tennessee standards. The defense contended that these files were legal in California and that the Tennessee court should just mind its own business. Of course, if Amateur Action's disk drives had been located in Mexico or Denmark, the postal agents would not have been able to get to them anyway. And if the files had been downloaded from an anonymous remailer, they would not even have known where to look.

This issue has also shown up dramatically in New Zealand, an isolated, island nation long accustomed to controlling flows across its borders. In 1994 the Technology and Crimes Reform Bill was introduced by a right-winger in the New Zealand parliament; it aimed, Canute-like, to roll back the tide of unwelcome bits that advanced telecommunications was bringing.[24] It proposed, among other things, to make transfer of "objectionable" material through telecommunications services illegal, and it made New Zealand network operators responsible for preventing New Zealand citizens from accessing foreign-based pornography bulletin boards. This proposal was viewed with understandable alarm by Waikato University, which is New Zealand's only Internet connection to the rest of the world.

You may sympathize with the attempts of local authorities to control kiddie porn, but how about suppression of dissident political speech? The Digital Freedom Network has dramatized the issue by setting up an online library with the sole purpose of providing Internet access to books that are banned in the authors' home countries.[25] This isn't an option for the literate good guys only, though; it would be just as easy for neo-Nazis to set up a server, somewhere carefully out of reach, for the crudest of hate propaganda. If nobody wanted to download their nasty stuff, they could simply deluge Usenet newsgroups with unsolicited postings. So *Fahrenheit 451* is becoming irrelevant; you can burn books, but not bits.[26]

Exports are as difficult to control as imports. On national security grounds, for example, the United States bans export of powerful cryptography software. But it is well known in the Internet community that copies of such software are available on openly accessible servers and can readily be downloaded by anyone with an Internet address anywhere in the world.

The rights that people think they have also become ambiguous when computer networks cross traditional jurisdictional boundaries. In Internet discussions of censorship and freedom of speech, for instance, participants often refer confidently to their "First Amendment rights." But whose constitution and whose amendment? The Internet community is an international one, with physical infrastructure and users scattered widely across different political and cultural units, so its norms and laws cannot simply be identified with those of people living within the borders of the United States.

TERRITORY / TOPOLOGY

While spatially defined power erodes in cyberspace, though, another kind of power arises to take its place — that of the system operators (sysops). Whoever runs a machine that serves as a network node can grant or deny user access to that node and can switch on or black out whatever subnetwork that node runs. Sysops can control the inflow of bits into a machine, decide which bits get stored there and which do not, determine which bits can be processed and in what ways, and control the outflow. So look to network topologies, not to jurisdictional maps, to discover patterns of control and power. In particular, look for strategic bottlenecks, the cyberspace Khyber Passes, through which many things flow but which can easily get cut off. These are the sites where real power is exerted.[27]

You will quickly see that operators of dial-in bulletin boards — like despotic rulers of walled city-states — can completely control them. Commercial online services like Compuserve and America Online also centralize power, but on a much larger scale, and they have to answer to very diverse and potentially fractious user communities. The private networks run by banks and other large business organizations are closed to outsiders and answer only to themselves.

The Internet, by contrast, is a huge, loose confederation of thousands of smaller, usually locally run, computer networks. Its structure is highly redundant (a feature ultimately deriving from its roots in the old ARPANET, which was deliberately given a distributed, redundant structure so that it could survive partial nuclear destruction and the knockout of military headquarters); there are normally many different ways to transmit a message from one node to another.[28] There are few Khyber Passes on the Internet, then, and there is no very effective way to grab control of it. Unlike banana republics, it does not have a clear center of authority to take over in a coup. It is a remarkable political invention — a very large-scale structure with significant built-in capacity to resist concentrations of power and authoritarian control.

But uncontrolled territory has its dangers. To protect themselves from the outlaws, interlopers, and subversives who may lurk on the wide-open Internet frontier, many commercial and governmental organizations have begun to create "firewalls" — secure computers interposed between their internal networks and the Internet outside. As in ancient walled cities, these organizations

then have narrow gates that allow traffic to go out but can be
defended against unwanted intrusions.

So a new logic has emerged. The great power struggles of cyberspace will be over network topology, connectivity, and access —
not the geographic borders and chunks of territory that have been
fought over in the past.

ELECTORAL POLITICS / ELECTRONIC POLLS

To Aristotle the idea of a placeless, borderless community would
have seemed very strange; it appeared self-evident to him that a
state — a self-governing political unit — had a definite, bounded
territory in which the citizens lived and over which they exerted
control. In *Politics* he devoted a section to enumerating the properties that this territory ideally should have: it should be productive
enough for self-sufficiency, large enough for the citizens to live
comfortably but in moderation, hard for hostile forces to invade,
easy for an expeditionary force to depart from, convenient for
surveillance, well situated in relation to sea and land transportation,
and well within reach of agricultural produce and of raw materials
needed for manufacturing processes.[29]

This classical view of the territorial state finds architectural expression in the government assembly buildings (usually augmented by
bureaucratic support structures) that traditionally have been erected
at the hearts of governed territories. (Nobody erects them outside,
except in the occasional special case of governments in exile.) So
a city has its city hall, a state has its state house, and a nation —
depending on its form of government — may have a Versailles, a
Westminster, a Kremlin, a White House and Congress, or whatever. At a larger scale, whole cities may be designated as state or
national capitals — special places for government business. In most

modern systems, the politicians who assemble in these places represent specific territories from whence they come.

Clearly the technological means are now emerging to replace these spatial and architectural arrangements with electronics and software, and it isn't hard to construct plausible arguments in favor of such a substitution. For a start, political assemblies could become virtual, with representatives connecting by computer network instead of sitting together in chambers. This is not such a big step; assembly chambers are already equipped with electronic systems for recording votes, and most of us watch the proceedings — if we watch them at all — on C-Span or on local cable. Such a rearrangement would be bad for things like fancy Washington restaurants, but it would keep politicians closer to their constituents, and it would save on transportation and accommodation costs.

However and wherever the power holders get together, though, there remain the more basic political questions of who holds power, whose interests are served by the power holders, and how these power holders are to be made accountable. Aristotle devoted a great deal of *Politics* to these issues. According to his teleological view, he argued that the state existed to serve the common good and that constitutions should therefore be judged according to whether the rulers served their own interests only or those of all the citizens. He then went on to describe and evaluate all the different types of constitutions that he could imagine — five types of kingship, four types of oligarchy, and four types of democracy.

As political theorists were quick to note when the discipline of cybernetics emerged in the 1940s and 1950s, these sorts of discussions can readily be recast in computational terms. You can, as Aristotle had pointed out, have various kinds of tyrannies in which control is exerted from the top and there is no effective feedback loop from the ruled to the rulers. Or you can put in feedback loops of some kind, so that the rulers feel the consequences of their actions and are prompted to attend to the common good. Elections, then, establish one important kind of feedback loop and opportunity for corrective action; if the rascals are not acting for the public good, the populace can throw them out.

But electoral mechanisms have some obvious limitations as control devices. They operate on a slow cycle, and their effects on specific policies may not be very sharply focused. This is, at least in part, an inevitable consequence of traditional electoral technology. When votes from large numbers of people scattered over wide areas must be collected and tabulated by manual means, the process always ends up being a sluggish, cumbersome, and expensive one. It just isn't practical to repeat it too frequently.

As telecommunications networks have developed, there has been growing flirtation with the idea of replacing old-fashioned voting booths and ballot boxes with electronic polling. In a cyberspace election, you might find the policies of candidates posted online, you might use your personal computer to go to a virtual polling place to cast your vote, and the votes might be tallied automatically in real time. Because all students have access to the on-campus Athena network, for example, MIT can conduct its student government elections in this way. There are, of course, potential problems with electronic stuffing of ballot boxes, but these can be handled through password control of access to the virtual ballot box or (better) through use of encryption technology to verify a voter's identity.

Other kinds of electronic feedback are evolving, too. For instance, as the Internet and commercial online service communities grew rapidly in the 1990s, American politicians quickly realized that they needed e-mail addresses. So you can now fire off your comments on the day's issues to *president@whitehouse.gov* or *vice.presi-*

dent@whitehouse.gov. The idea quickly spread to other parts of the world; in summer 1994 Poland's prime minister, Waldemar Pawlak, went online at *prime_minister@urm.gov.pl.*[30] And I once tried sending some suggestions on reproductive rights to *pope@vatican.com,* but it just turned out to be the address of a hacker playing a prank. Anyway, the pontiff logs in wirelessly to quite another place.

Electronic feedback can even be swift enough, potentially, to support real-time (or at least very fast) direct democracy on a large scale.[31] Populist demagogues like Ross Perot have proffered visions of sitting in front of your two-way television, watching debates, and bypassing the politicians by immediately, electronically recording your response. The network presents the packaged alternatives. Vote with your remote!

Grizzled old operators still like to assure us that "all politics is local." But in the cyberspace era, things may be very different. You do not have to buy into Perot's appallingly reductionist view of political discourse to realize that cyberspace has the potential to change political institutions and mechanisms fundamentally; it opens up ways of assembling and communicating with dispersed political constituencies, new opportunities for instigating and formulating issues, and mechanisms for providing decisions and feedback at a much faster pace than in the past.

BANISHMENT / SYSOP BLACKLIST

Of course the holders of power cannot get through cyberspace to the bodies of those over whom they hold sway (though this is a matter of interface design and may change),[32] so the usual means of maintaining power through potential or actual violence are not available when cyberspace communities are geographically widely distributed or cross jurisdictional boundaries. The ancient strategy of banishment has been revived instead: just as the emperor Augustus banished Ovid from Rome to the desolate shores of the Black

Sea (for adultery compounded by a salacious poem instigating it), system operators can kick you off the Net. Your name is removed from a control list and you lose your "access privileges."[33] What's even worse, your name may end up on the sysop's permanent blacklist. This is what will happen to you if you don't pay your America Online bill, if you try to play Ovid on Prodigy, or if you seriously offend the system manager of your Internet gateway. If you just use the Net casually, for recreational purposes, banishment may not hurt you very much. But for scientists and scholars who depend on network access for crucial information, for business people who conduct profitable transactions in cyberspace, and for those whose social life depends on cyberspace encounters and assignations, banishment is a severe punishment, and the threat of it can be an effective form of discipline.

Verbal violence is another possibility, and cyberspace offers no impediment to that. Indeed, electronic communication seems to encourage it. The extraordinarily common practice of "flaming" — sending abusive, invective-filled e-mail messages or bulletin board postings probably reflects a need to maintain customary power that would otherwise be challenged in a new domain where the threat of physical violence does not work very well. It can also be a way of grabbing power by creating fear — particularly fear of humiliation in public forums. Bosses flame subordinates. Old hands flame clueless newcomers. Men flame women. The flame wars that frequently erupt, like Wild West gunfights between cattlemen and sheepmen, are contests for control of territory on the cyberspace frontier. Since there is no direct threat of physical retaliation, the verbal violence often takes extreme forms; people routinely fire off remarks that would get them decked in a bar, and frustrated recipients shoot back in kind.[34]

If a power holder cannot inflict direct punishment on someone, or feels somehow constrained from doing so, he or she can get to that person indirectly by seizing or destroying the person's property. So legal systems use fines and confiscations as alternatives to confining the body, inflicting pain, and execution. This strategy is also effective in cyberspace, since electronic information — the form of valuable property that exists there — is very vulnerable to seizure and destruction; if you transgress against system operators, you risk not only getting banished, but also having your files erased.

In variants on time-honored strategies for contesting power, though, all of these techniques can be turned back on the rulers — and on occasion have been, with increasing effectiveness, as cyberspace communities have grown and diversified. Hacker break-ins to computer systems are the subversive answer to exclusion and banishment. System operators "legitimately" erase files; computer "criminals" deploy their software viruses and worms to equivalent effect. In cyberspace, as elsewhere, the means of maintaining power are also the means of resisting and usurping it.

Surveillance / Electronic Panopticon

Though the fashion for Foucault has come and gone, the PoMo *maître* has left us with the indelible realization that power and surveillance are tightly bound up together. He repeatedly portrayed society as a giant panopticon, in which power holders exert surveillance over the rest and in which subjects' *awareness* of constant surveillance is a reminder that punishment awaits if they step out of line. The rulers would know, and they would respond.

It is not surprising, then, that a traditional role of architecture has been not only to make efficient surveillance possible, but also publicly to *represent* the presence of surveillance. Jeremy Bentham's own panopticon prison design is not unique, but only one of the most extreme and vividly diagrammatic examples. After all, civic and institutional buildings are normally constructed by those in power. So we see prominent watchtowers on the walls of old cities and of modern jails, monumental police headquarters buildings bristling with electronic antennae in city centers (look at Parker Center in downtown Los Angeles), receptionist and guard desks conspicuously placed in building lobbies everywhere, and even little signs saying "Police take notice."

As the electronic era dawned, George Orwell presciently anticipated that telecommunications devices would take over these roles; in the world of *1984* the television monitor became an ever-present instrument of surveillance, and the displayed face of Big Brother was a constant, graphic reminder that he was, indeed, watching. But Orwell did not bother to think through the technical details, and this scheme would not really have worked — not with the primitive electronics that Orwell knew about, anyway. Where would Big Brother have put all the corresponding monitors on the receiving end? Where would he have found the labor force to watch them all? How would he have sifted through and collated all that information?

What actually happened was far more subtle and insidious. Instead of one Big Brother, we got a vast swarm of Little Brothers. Every computer input device became a potential recorder of our actions. Every digital transaction potentially left fingerprints somewhere in cyberspace. Huge databases of personal information began to accumulate. And the collation problem was solved; efficient software could be written to collect fragments of information from multiple locations in cyberspace and put them together to form remarkably complete pictures of how we were conducting our lives. We entered the era of dataveillance.[35]

The last time I came face-to-face with the Little Brother dataveillance force was in a car salesman's cubicle. In response to the Honda hawker's two-finger typed command, a jittering old printer spewed out a TRW credit report, a minutely detailed listing of all my credit transactions and transgressions, going back years and years. Many sources had been combed and correlated electronically to put it all together: the databases of banks, stores, collection agencies, credit unions, insurance companies, motor vehicle agencies, magazine subscription services, and a lot more.[36] It was an impressive performance; TRW's electronically mediated surveillance had never faltered, and it had not missed anything. That printed report was as vivid a demonstration of power as any face peering out from a display screen.

But this is just the beginning; our lives have been leaving increasingly complete and detailed traces in cyberspace as two-way electronic communications devices have proliferated and diversified. Telephones were the first such devices to find widespread use; they soon yielded telephone company billing data — records of when, where, and by whom calls were made. Then bank ATM machines and point-of-sale terminals in retail stores began to produce transaction records. As personal computers were plugged into commercial online networks, they too began to create electronic trails.

There is more of this to come. As switched video networks become extensively used for everyday purposes — shopping, banking, selecting movies, social contact, political assembly — they potentially will grab and keep much more detailed portraits of private lives than have ever been made before. And wearable devices — ones that continuously monitor your medical condition, for example, or perhaps the cybersex suits that some journalists have avidly imagined — may construct the most up-close and intimate of records.

Life in cyberspace generates electronic trails as inevitably as soft ground retains footprints; that, in itself, is not the worrisome thing. But where will digital information about your contacts and activities reside? Who will have access to it and under what circumstances? Will information of different kinds be kept separately, or will there be ways to assemble it electronically to create close and detailed pictures of your life? These are the questions that we will face with increasing urgency as we shift more and more of our daily activities into the digital, electronic sphere.

Contention about the limits of privacy and surveillance is not new, but the terms and stakes of the central questions are rapidly being redefined. Isolated hermits can keep to themselves and don't have to keep up appearances, but city dwellers have always had to accept that they will see and be seen. In return for the benefits of urban life, they tolerate some level of visibility and some possibility of surveillance — some erosion of their privacy. Architecture, laws, and customs maintain and represent whatever balance has been struck. As we construct and inhabit cyberspace communities, we will have to make and maintain similar bargains — though they will be embodied in software structures and electronic access controls rather than in architectural arrangements. And we had better get them right; since electronic data collection and digital collation techniques are so much more powerful than any that could be deployed in the past, they provide the means to create the ultimate Foucaultian dystopia.[37]

THE POLITICAL ECONOMY OF CYBERSPACE

All this migration of social, economic, and political activity to cyberspace will force us to rethink traditional relationships between the civic and the urban. Latin, as Fustel de Coulanges observed in his great work on the ancient city, distinguishes between the terms *civitas* and *urbs*. Families or tribes who joined together because they shared the same religious beliefs, social organization, form of government, and modes of production created *civitas* — a community that was not necessarily related to any particular place or construction. But when such a unit chose a particular site and founded a city in which to dwell — as Rome was founded on the seven hills — an *urban* settlement resulted. So urban space became the territory of the civic formation, and civic principles determined the spatial configuration of the city. Choice of site, performance of the foundation ritual, and organization of the layout were seen as such fundamentally important acts that they were traditionally ascribed to the community's gods and mythic heroes.

Today, this ancient idea — reflected in the *Oxford* definition of a community as a "body of people living in one place, district, or country" — is eroding; a community may now find its place in cyberspace. The new sort of site is not some suitable patch of earth but a computer to which members may connect from wherever they happen to be. The foundation ritual is not one of marking boundaries and making obeisance to the gods, but of allocating disk space and going online. And the new urban design task is not one of configuring buildings, streets, and public spaces to meet the needs and aspirations of the *civitas,* but one of writing computer code and deploying software objects to create virtual places and electronic interconnections between them. Within these places, social contacts will be made, economic transactions will be carried out, cultural life will unfold, surveillance will be enacted, and power will be exerted.

As these soft cities develop, we will need to consider not only their urban design — the places and interconnections that they provide, and their look and feel — but also their civic character. We will have to figure out how to make cyberspace communities work in just, equitable, and satisfying ways.

So far, there are no definitive answers to the questions that this task poses, but as this windshield survey along the infobahn has shown, there are at least a few emerging models to consider. The commercial online systems have developed, until now, as company towns — centrally controlled enterprises that own the infrastructure and try to make money by renting space to information and service providers, by charging access fees to subscribers, and (like broadcast media) by selling advertising. Some smaller, dial-in systems like the WELL belong to the communitarian, utopian tradition; they have relied on generating a shared commitment to the common good and on informal, barter systems of information exchange. Discussions of a national information infrastructure raise the possibility that the essential infrastructure elements, like streets and sewers, might be constructed and run by government monopolies and paid for with tax dollars. And the Internet demonstrates the possibility of a multilayered, heterogeneous, decentralized system in which the constituent communities organize themselves, run their local affairs, and pay their bills in many different ways.

As communities increasingly find their common ground in cyberspace rather than on *terra firma,* these models will be debated, extended, and transformed. The fundamental questions of cyberspace's political economy will urgently be contested. Who plays, who pays, and how is this decided? How is trade to be conducted, and how is intellectual property to be managed and protected? What is the role of agents, and what sorts of regulation might these software slaves require? How should communities define their boundaries, and how might they maintain their norms within these boundaries? What are the legitimate forms of power? How might political discourse be constructed?

These are questions worthy of an online Aristotle. If he were around to frequent the electronic Lyceum, you would probably find some pretty lively discussion at *alt.Politics.*

7

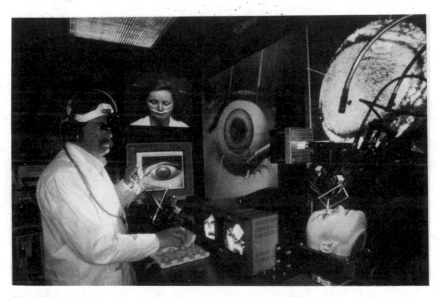

The information infrastructure potentially redistributes access to services and opportunities: a prototype system for delivering surgical expertise to remote locations.

During the nineteenth and twentieth centuries, cities have been transformed by successive waves of transportation and communications technology. At each stage, new combinations of buildings, transportation systems, and communication networks have served the needs of the inhabitants. Now, as the infobahn takes over a widening range of functions, the roles of inhabited structures and transportation systems are shifting once again, fresh urban patterns are forming, and we have the opportunity to rethink received ideas of what buildings and cities are, how they can be made, and what they are really for. The challenge is to do this right — to get us to the good bits.

GETTING TO THE GOOD BITS

1835: PRE-INDUSTRIAL SETTLEMENTS

"This will be a place for a village," intoned the explorer John Batman when he encountered Port Phillip Bay in 1835, as I recall from the Australian history that I learned so long ago in dusty country schoolrooms with the songs of magpies swirling in on the scorching, eucalyptus-laden breeze. We would take out our red plastic templates to trace maps of the island continent and its straggling river systems into our blue-lined exercise books, then we would meticulously mark the tracks of inland trailblazers and coastal navigators, locating the settlements that followed and inscribing the dates.

Much later, when I learned the age-old distinction between *civitas* and *urbs,* I realized that we had been rehearsing our own particular foundation myths — the ritualized tales of how our wandering ancestors had chosen sites and constructed places for their communities. We schoolchildren in the bush learned of the heroes who selected the spots, of the settlers who came to these places, and of how the first, rough tracks and shelters were laid out upon the freshly cleared ground. We were told of convict settlements and ports for communities of whalers and sealers along the coasts, of the gold-rush towns and agricultural centers that had sprung up in the interior, of how the railroad and telegraph systems had spawned remote and desolate villages, and of how merchant, industrial, and administrative cities had grown at favored locations in the emerging transportation network. And we heard how colonial bureaucrats and military officers — Hoddle, Light, and others — had plunked down the surveyed street grids that introduced the beginnings of urban form and order to the scrubby brown land.

1 9 5 6 : T H E C O M M U T E R C I T Y

By 1956, when I first made the long, slow rail journey to the distant big city — for the Olympics in Melbourne — industrial capitalism had firmly taken hold and the postwar immigrants were pouring in. Some hours after meat pie and tea at the Ballarat railway refreshment rooms (a beer for Dad), the grimy train steamed first through a ring of suburban housing, then penetrated what seemed an interminable zone of factories and warehouses to reach the heart of the metropolis. There I found department stores and shopping arcades, theaters, grand old hotels, government offices, the headquarters of banks and insurance companies, the fancy professional consulting rooms of Collins Street, crowds, and foreign voices. It was all there. And every day the trams and trains and streams of cars would wash a huge tide of workers into the city in the morning, then — with a brief pause for thirsty workers to grab a

drink at the pub (a custom known locally as the six o'clock swill)
— would suck them out to suburbia again in the evening.

All these patterns and rhythms were generated by the need to put
bodies in particular places, at particular times, for particular purposes. The convict settlements were intended to remove the un-
desirable and inconvenient to the antipodes — as far from English
soil as possible, at places that had been picked out for their practi-
cality as ports and their supposed potential for self-supporting agriculture. The gold-rush towns exploded into existence at just those
spots where miners could dig the precious metal from the ground,
and the cattle and sheep men were drawn to water and grazing
lands. Often these special places were far from each other, and
certainly they were all remote from the rest of the world —
connected by lengthy and tenuous transportation routes along
which passengers, products, and information slowly and sporadi-
cally flowed, their inhabitants had no way to escape the prison
house of distance. By mid-twentieth century in the coastal capitals,
the space of the city itself was subdivided into specialized places to
live, places to go to work, and places to assemble for shopping and
entertainment, all interconnected by roads and railway networks
for moving bodies back and forth. And it mattered where you came
from — the tree-lined pleasances of South Yarra or the grubby
streets of Brunswick, Sydney, or the bush.

In the sixties, geography was destiny still, so many of my generation
left the vast, isolated southern continent to be closer to the centers
of things.

1994: TELEPRESENCE

Fast forward. The year is now 1994, and I am typing this text on
a computer in my office at MIT. On the same screen, there is a
video window open to the design studio upstairs where my students

are working, and there are additional windows to studios at universities in St. Louis, upstate New York, Vancouver, Hong Kong, and Barcelona. There is a small video camera on my desk, so that the students can also see me at work. We are all interconnected by the Internet, and the students in these different locations and time zones are working together on proposals for some new housing in an old area of Shanghai. Through their computer workstations, the students and their instructors can exchange CAD models and rendered images of proposals, get answers to queries about site and program, and discuss and criticize each other's work. For the moment, at least, we scattered souls have become an electronically linked virtual community. Bodily location is no longer an issue; for me, the students in Hong Kong are as much a part of it as are those to be found within walking distance of my office.

We have reinvented the human habitat. Back when it took many months for an exchange of letters between an isolated Australian settlement and a foreign city, most of a citizen's interactions were necessarily with other inhabitants of that same settlement. Your community consisted of your close neighbors; you could love it or you could leave it. But as transportation and communications capabilities improved in the industrial era, maintaining contact with widely dispersed friends and family became much easier, and it became possible to participate actively in communities of interest that were not tied to your hometown. In the two centuries from the first convict fleet's arrival in Botany Bay to the formation of the Internet — 1788 to 1988 — the preindustrial relationship of *civitas* to *urbs* was radically restructured. Today, as telepresence augments and sometimes substitutes for physical presence, and as more and more business and social interactions shift into cyberspace, we are finding that accessibility depends even less on propinquity, and community has come increasingly unglued from geography. Our network connections are becoming as important to us as our bodily locations.

Cyberspace is opening up, and the rush to claim and settle it is on. We are entering an era of electronically extended bodies living at the intersection points of the physical and virtual worlds, of occupation and interaction through telepresence as well as through physical presence, of mutant architectural forms that emerge from the telecommunications-induced fragmentation and recombination of traditional architectural types, and of new, soft cities that parallel, complement, and sometimes compete with our existing urban concentrations of brick, concrete, and steel.

For designers and planners, the task of the twenty-first century will be to build the bitsphere — a worldwide, electronically mediated environment in which networks are everywhere, and most of the artifacts that function within it (at every scale, from nano to global) have intelligence and telecommunications capabilities. It will overlay and eventually succeed the agricultural and industrial landscapes that humankind has inhabited for so long.

This unprecedented, hyperextended habitat will transcend national boundaries; the increasingly dense and widespread connectivity that it supplies will quickly create opportunities — the first in the history of humankind — for planning and designing truly worldwide communities. Just as the ancient *polis* provided an agora, markets, and theaters for those living within its walls, the twenty-first-century bitsphere will require a growing number of virtual gathering places, exchanges, and entertainment spots for its plugged-in populace. Just as architects have traditionally designed schools, hospitals, and other service facilities to meet the needs of surrounding local areas, bitsphere planners and designers will structure the channels, resources, and interfaces of educational and medical service delivery systems for much more extended constituencies. Commercial, entertainment, educational, and health care organizations will use these new delivery systems and virtual places to operate, cooperate, and compete on a global scale.

We will need rules for this emerging game. Like more familiar social and political units, international bitsphere communities will urgently require appropriate constitutions, institutions, public policies, and laws; perhaps there will be a specialized law of cyberspace, as there is now a law of the sea. At the same time, established, territorially defined nations, states, regions, and cities will have to adapt their pre-bitsphere structures and customs to the new context — one in which borders no longer have their old meaning, rights and powers may not be defined by spatial boundaries, property cannot be protected in traditional ways, and much of the economic, social, and cultural action has been attracted to the upstart venues of cyberspace.

Nations that seek to remain economically competitive and to provide high living standards for their citizens will race to embark on their National Information Infrastructure projects as, in the past, they have invested in their ports and shipping fleets, railroad networks, and highway systems. And as they do so, they will have to resolve fundamental questions about the political economy of cyberspace; the answers that they reach will largely determine the kinds of nations that they become. Democratic ideals (and the lessons of the telephone system) suggest that they should strive to provide universal access — affordable, ubiquitously present, high-bandwidth service to all their citizens. If equality of opportunity and symmetry of participation are valued, then all classes of users (not just privileged groups and institutions) should be able to create as well as receive information; this means that the infrastructure has to provide two-way digital pipes and allow anyone to set up a server. If bottom-up community development efforts and entrepreneurial enterprise are to be encouraged, then the infrastructure must have a carefully crafted open architecture; it should allow a wide range of hardware companies, software developers, network service providers, content providers, and users to produce and integrate components which extend and add value to the system. And if the infrastructure is to encourage national coherence rather than a new kind of balkanization, then its development must be guided by policies and standards that assure interoperability between all the subnetworks of the national system.

These national information infrastructures will not come cheap, and policy makers will face the difficult question of how to pay for them. The various possible answers have profoundly differing social consequences, so the policy debates are likely to be contentious ones. Some will argue, from positions grounded on ideals of social justice, that universal access and attention to the public good should be guaranteed by treating national information infrastructures as public utilities paid for with tax dollars. Others will claim that only the private sector can mobilize the resources needed to construct these infrastructures quickly and run them efficiently and that private-sector service providers will therefore have to be motivated by opportunities for profits from toll charges and advertising sales. In the end, cyberspace development — much like real estate development — will probably progress through a complex and evolving blend of public policies and investments with private-sector responses to emerging opportunities.

Does development of national and international information infrastructures, and the consequent shift of social and economic activity to cyberspace, mean that existing cities will simply fragment and collapse? Or does Paris have something that telepresence cannot match? Does Rome have an answer to *Neuromancer?* Most of us would bet our bottom bits that the reserves of resilience and adaptability that have allowed great cities to survive (in changed form) the challenges of industrialization and the automobile will similarly enable them to adapt to the bitsphere. Though immersion in electronically propelled bits will progressively reduce our reliance on bodily presence and material exchange, thus altering the ways in which we use physical space and weakening many of the activity linkages that now hold large urban agglomerations together, there is no reason to think that this novel condition will make us indifferent to our immediate surroundings or suddenly eliminate our desire for face-to-face human contact in congenial settings. We will still care about where we are, and we will still want company. So cities and towns will probably find opportunities to restructure themselves — to regroup housing, workplaces, and service facilities into reinvigorated small-scale neighborhoods (both urban and rural) that are effectively nourished by strong electronic links to a wider world, but simultaneously prize their differences from other places, their local institutions and hangouts, and their unique ambiences and customs. A community's capacity to connect globally can yield renewed opportunity for its citizens — freed from the need to seek employment and services in distant urban centers — to know their neighbors and to participate in local affairs.

As the development of pioneering campus and community networks has already suggested, there will be an important role here for local subnetworks of the national and international systems — electronic Main Streets that provide places for citizens to present themselves in their communities, to exchange greetings and gossip with neighbors, and to transact local business. Bitsphere civic design will encompass not only traditional matters of roads and sidewalks, sewers, and land-use zoning, but also development of local network infrastructure and creation of electronic venues for local communication and interaction.

By redirecting access to services and opportunities, the growing information infrastructure has the potential to create winners and losers on a vast scale. It is pleasant to imagine a nation of networked Aspens and cyberspaced Santa Monicas peopled by convivial, bicycle-riding locals, but the obvious danger is that such restructuring will instead produce electronic Jakartas — well-connected, well-serviced, fortified enclaves of privilege surrounded by miserable hyperghettoes, where investments in information infrastructure and appliances are not made, electronically delivered services do not reach, and few economic opportunities are to be found. The poor could be left with the obsolete and decaying urban remnants and isolated rural settlements that the more privileged no longer need. Surely the most fundamental challenge in building the bitsphere will be to deploy access according to principles of social equity — not in ways that heighten the privilege of the haves and further marginalize the have-nots.

Within bitsphere communities, there will be subnetworks at a smaller scale still   that of architecture. Increasingly, computers will meld seamlessly into the fabric of buildings and buildings themselves will become computers — the outcome of a long evolution. Pre-industrial buildings were not much more than supporting skeletons and enclosing skins. With the Industrial Revolution, they acquired increasingly complicated mechanical physiologies; soon they were routinely equipped with water supply and sewage systems, heating and air-conditioning systems, electrical systems, safety systems, and more. Now they are getting electronic nervous systems — network connections, cabling in the woodwork, and information appliances. As the speed at which bits zip around a building approaches that at which they are moved inside today's computers, as different sorts of specialized sensors and input devices harvest bits at arbitrary locations, as processors are embedded wherever they happen to be needed, and as all the various displays and appliances are integrated into building-wide, digitally controlled systems, it will become meaningless to ask where the smart electronics end and the dumb construction begins; computers will burst out of their boxes, walls will be wired, and the architectural works of the bitsphere will be less structures with chips than robots with foundations.

Architects will increasingly confront practical choices between providing for bodily presence and relying on telepresence. They will be forced to explore the proper respective roles of physically constructed hardware and symbolically encoded software, and of actual space and virtual places. And eventually they will find new ways to accommodate human needs by recombining transformed fragments of traditional building types in a matrix of digital telecommunication systems and reorganized circulation and transportation patterns. From the sidelines, no doubt, technoromantic theoreticians will egg them on to Gibsonian gestures of dematerialization and radical renunciation of traditional architectural means, while materiality chauvinists will provide ringing denunciations of a world that they see going to hell in a handheld device.

And finally, there will be the intimate bits. Just as clothing has traditionally formed a first interface to the physical world, so our personal electronic devices and bodynets will become interfaces between flesh and nervous system and the bitsphere. Hand-held remote control devices will be used to interact with digital televisions and other information devices. Personal digital assistants and laptop computers will wirelessly exchange bits with the surrounding infrastructure. Body-mounted and implanted medical monitoring devices will transmit data to environmental control systems. Miniature storage devices will hold vital medical records, identification, and digital cash. Our electronic accouterments will range from headphones to sensor gloves and the latest fashions in smart sneakers. And their designers will create the most immediate, private digital environments — our personal cyberspace.

Networks at these different levels will all have to link up somehow; the body net will be connected to the building net, the building net to the community net, and the community net to the global net. From gesture sensors worn on our bodies to the worldwide infrastructure of communications satellites and long-distance fiber, the elements of the bitsphere will finally come together to form one densely interwoven system within which the knee bone is connected to the I-bahn.

The uncertainties and dangers of the bitsphere frontier are great, but it is a place of new opportunity and hope. So forget the global couch-potato patches that Marshall McLuhan surveyed back in the sixties. *This* will be the place for a global village.

1. For an overview of the process of fiber-optic network installation, see Andrew Kupfer, "The Race to Rewire America," *Fortune,* April 19, 1993, 42–61. The converging futures of computer networks, cable TV networks, and telephone networks are explored in detail in Gary Stix, "Domesticating Cyberspace," *Scientific American* 269: 2 (August 1993): 100–10.

2. Development of the worldwide telecommunications infrastructure began in 1837, when the telegraph was demonstrated and patented. The telephone followed in 1876. Long-distance telegraph and telephone networks had developed by the dawn of the twentieth century, and the technology of wireless telegraphy was emerging. By the 1950s extensive analog telecommunications networks employed wire, cable, and micro-

N O T E S

wave links together with crossbar switching technology. In the 1960s digital telecommunications systems began to supplant the older analog ones, and the first communications satellites were put into service. Fiber-optic cables and ISDN (Integrated Services Digital Network) lines became increasingly commonplace in the 1980s. By mid-1991 the local cable television company was providing me with direct access to the Internet computer network from my home in Cambridge, Massachusetts, and it was clear that existing, largely separate, telephone, radio, television, and data networks would eventually evolve into a worldwide, broadband, digital service. Politicians and journalists began to talk about the emergence of an Information Superhighway system.

3. Cable links are mostly underground and in building walls, wireless links are completely invisible, and most installations of digital telecommunications equipment are small and inconspicuous.

1. The Parisian *flâneur* made his literary debut in Baudelaire's famous essay "The Painter of Modern Life" (1863). He was a man of the boulevards: he strolled them to observe the life of the great city and by so doing also put himself on display.

2. The Greek agora is the prototype urban public space. In the ancient Greek city, the agora was a central, open space where public life was enacted. Having an agora was essential to being a city rather than merely a settlement.

3. After being overrun and destroyed by the Persians in 494 B.C., the Ionian city of Miletos was rebuilt, beginning in 479 B.C., according to a master plan by the Milesian architect Hippodamos. It was sited on a rocky peninsula on the Aegean coast of what is now Turkey. Streets were laid out in a regular grid, and there was a magnificent agora in the center, adjacent to the harbor. Aristotle credited Hippodamos with being the inventor of "the art of planning cities."

4. The software performs the basic functions of storing messages at some central location as they arrive, then forwarding them to the addressee's personal computer or workstation when requested. Voice mail and video mail systems operate in similar ways.

5. Sometimes a domain that is closely associated with a particular group — for example *media@mit* — does acquire a certain cachet. As network usage grows, it may be that some access providers will attempt to distinguish themselves by providing premium service (faster machines, fancier interfaces) and trade on their snob value. But at least for now the basic point remains valid: logical connection matters much more than physical location. The compendium *E-Mail Addresses of the Rich and Famous* (Reading, MA: Addison-Wesley, 1994) does not define any particular cyberspace neighborhood.

6. Finger files are maintained by many of the host computers on the Internet. (Some hosts, for security or privacy reasons, do not provide access

to them.) Internet users can, for example, finger me by typing *finger wjm@mit.edu*. This yields my full name, mailing address, and phone number — just as if they looked me up in the printed MIT phone directory. If they are resourceful and knowledgeable, they can construct a fairly detailed description of me (or practically anybody else who uses Internet) by piecing together fragments of information from various accessible databases.

7. For example, the *San Jose Mercury News* maintains an online database of personal ads (not that you will find me on this one). Give the command "Search RSVP personals" and you will be greeted with the message, "Type words that describe what you are looking for, then click List Ads. For example, 'men and non-smoker.'"

8. For information on the Usenet Oracle, send e-mail to *oracle@cs.indiana.edu* with the word "help" in the "Subject" line.

9. See Erving Goffman's classic *The Presentation of Self in Everyday Life* (New York: Doubleday, 1959) for a discussion of the many and complex ways in which we acquire information about general socioeconomic status, competence, trustworthiness, attitude, and so on in face-to-face interactions.

10. Even before text became digital, printed text created some space for these games. George Eliot and Henry Handel Richardson played them with panache. But the network greatly expands that space.

11. Some early published stories of this sort of thing quickly attained the status of cyberspace morality tales. A 1985 *Ms.* magazine story by Lindsy Van Gelder, for example, told the story of "Joan," a disabled older woman who participated in the Compuserve network's "Between the Sexes" online conference. "Joan" was eventually unmasked, to the shock and dismay of many of the other conference participants, as a middle-aged male psychiatrist. Then, in summer 1993, the news media reported widely on "The Case of the Cybercad" on the WELL (a popular Bay Area online conferencing system). After he teleromanced several women at the same time (without telling them of the others), the women tumbled to his

deceptive game and publicly denounced him in a WELL conference space. These tales recall similar ones from the early days of the telephone, when "phonies" began to take advantage of the telephone's elimination of visual cues, and people's inexperience in dealing with this, to set up swindles.

12. Students of cyberspace culture might, then, do well to take a close look at the gay studies literature.

13. Such agents are discussed in detail in the "Intelligent Agents" special issue of *Communications of the ACM* 37: 7 (July 1994). In 1994 the idea began to go commercial in a significant way; for example, General Magic introduced the Telescript language intended for programming practical software agents. See John Markoff, "Hopes and Fears on New Computer Organisms," *The New York Times,* Thursday, January 6, 1994, D1, D5.

14. Joseph Bates, "The Role of Emotion in Believable Agents," *Communications of the ACM* 37: 7 (July 1994): 122–25.

15. Apple Computer's famous promotional videotape *The Knowledge Navigator* provided an early dramatization of this idea. It featured a bow-tied agent called Phil, who looked a bit like a talking passport photo and who supposedly performed librarian and resource-management tasks.

16. There is now a technical answer of a sort. We can use encryption techniques to put verifiable digital "signatures" on electronic documents. But this does not alter the basic fact that telecommunication distances us from the flesh-and-blood bodies of those with whom we communicate and puts constructed electronic masks in their place.

17. This already happens with machines. The existence of once-popular but now obsolete types of computer terminals, such as teletypes and DEC VT-100s, is regularly simulated by software running on more up-to-date hardware.

18. Mitch Kapor (in an e-mail note after reading a manuscript draft) has chided me for being a bit silly about this. He may be right. Many of the early, grand promises of artificial intelligence have gone unfulfilled and

will continue to be unfulfilled unless there are spectacular breakthroughs of a kind that do not seem imminent, so we cannot expect to get to Gibsonian silicon immortality by extrapolation of current technology. But it is certainly worth noting, at least, that existence on the Net radically extends the kind of pseudo-immortality that authors gain from having their books published.

19. For the early history of asynchronous communication systems (using runners, chains of men with loud voices, pigeons, drums and horns, fire, semaphore, ships, the Pony Express, and so on), see Prakash Chakravati, "Communications from Cave Messages to Mail Messages," *IEEE Power Engineering Review* 12: 9 (September 1992): 29–31.

20. In *Technics and Civilization* (New York: Harcourt Brace Jovanovich, 1934) Lewis Mumford dated the synchronous city back to the thirteenth century, when monasteries introduced mechanical clocks, began to ring out the hours, and so started to impose orderly routines on urban life.

21. There is a growing literature on the relationship between telecommunications and the use of time in modern urban societies. See D. Gross, "Space, Time, and Modern Culture," *Telos* 50 (1981): 59–78; D. Gross, "Temporality and the Modern State," *Theory and Society* 14 (1985): 53–82; A. Kellerman, *Time, Space, and Society: Geographical Societal Perspectives* (Dordrecht: Kluwer, 1989); A. Kellerman, "The Decycling of Time and the Reorganization of Urban Space," *Cultural Dynamics* 4 (1991): 38–54; G. Raulet, "The New Utopia: Communication Technologies," *Telos* 87 (1991): 39–58.

22. The first teleport was developed by the Port Authority of New York and New Jersey in the late 1970s; Manhattan office buildings were connected via fiber-optic links to a telecommunications park in New Jersey. On teleports generally, see A. D. Lipman, A. D. Sugarman, and R. F. Cushman, eds., *Teleports and the Intelligent City* (Homewood, IL: Dow Jones-Irwin, 1986).

23. L. Qvortrup, "The Nordic Telecottages: Community Teleservice Centers for Rural Regions," *Telecommunications Policy* 13 (1990): 59–68.

24. For a brief introduction to the geography of communications satellites, see A. Kellerman, "Microwave and Satellite Communications," *Telecommunications and Geography* (London: Belhaven, 1993), pp. 38–47.

25. For a lively analysis of the issues involved here, see Nicholas Negroponte, "The Bit Police: Will the FCC Regulate Licenses to Radiate Bits?," *Wired* 1:2 (May/June 1993): 112.

26. As I wrote these words, despite endless talk in the popular press about the Information Superhighway, most American schoolrooms did not even have telephones.

27. Actually, of course, we are talking about a great many more bits. From a telecommunications viewpoint, intimacy is a matter of using all sensory modalities and opening up the bandwidth as far as possible. Conversely, stripteases (look, don't touch) and other rituals of erotic titillation often depend on shutting down a few sensory channels.

28. Bandwidth becomes particularly important here since the rough telecommunications rule of thumb is that good video requires about a thousand times as much bandwidth as speech. A picture is truly worth a thousand words.

29. One current approach is to combine a gesture-sensing glove with arrays of tiny switches known as tactors. When the tactors are stimulated by a current, they press on the fingertips. Pneumatic cylinders that provide variable resistance to the fingers as air pressure is regulated by computer have also been tried. Yet another approach is to employ servomotor-driven joysticks that vibrate to simulate movement across rough and bumpy surfaces, and push back when solid objects or force fields are encountered. At a larger scale, flight simulators and motion-based amusement rides use hydraulic rams to accelerate riders over short distances and so subject them to g-forces similar to those experienced in moving vehicles. Perhaps the most effective early application of force feedback, though, was in the Atari videogame *Hard Drivin',* which transmitted through a steering wheel the feel of a racecar in motion.

30. For example, stationary exercise bicycles have incorporated increasingly sophisticated computer monitoring of the user's physical response, together with automatic adjustment of the level of difficulty of the simulated terrain. And NEC's "virtual skiing" laboratory in Tokyo has developed a system that senses head position, leg movements, and pole movements, as well as blood flow and stress; it simulates actual slopes and adjusts them according to the user's ability. See Kimiko Eastham, "Everything but the Broken Bones," *Wired* 1: 3 (July/August 1993): 29.

31. Postmodern prostitution is a pretty hackneyed fantasy by now (though journalists never seem to tire of pop-eyed speculation about it); Frederik Pohl explored it in his 1966 short story "Day Million." For a survey of interactive computer porn in the 1990s, see John Tierney, "Porn, the Low-Slung Engine of Progress," *The New York Times,* Sunday, January 9, 1994, section 2, pp. 1, 18.

32. For a comprehensive survey of the relevant technologies, see Grigore Burdea and Philippe Coiffet, *Virtual Reality Technology* (New York: John Wiley, 1994).

33. Paul Virilio, *The Lost Dimension* (New York: Semiotext(e), 1991), p. 60.

34. Once again, pen > sword. This word does not have a respectable technical pedigree, but was introduced by William Gibson in his 1984 novel *Neuromancer.* Many old computer hands detest it for the conceptual vulgarities that it has come to connote. But it has won out against all the plausible alternatives and has succeeded in taking possession of its semantic niche, so I shall use it.

35. A literary subgenre, analogous to the western pulp novel, has already developed to chronicle the tales of this territory. Basic sources on the topic are John Perry Barlow, "Crime and Puzzlement" (June 8, 1990) and "Crime and Puzzlement Part 2" (July 21, 1990), available by FTP from the Electronic Frontier Foundation (*eff@well.sf.ca.us*).

36. Most of the research and fact-checking for this book was done by browsing, searching, and retrieving information in this way. My research assistant, Anne Beamish, spent most of her time surfing the Net to search library catalogues, bibliographies, and databases and to download papers, news stories, and press releases.

3 CYBORG CITIZENS

1. In the seventeenth century, Robert Hooke clearly saw this coming. In the preface to *Micrographia* (1665) he wrote: "The next care to be taken, in respect of the Senses, is a supplying of their infirmities with *Instruments,* and as it were, the adding of *artificial Organs* to the natural. . . . And as *Glasses* have highly promoted our seeing, so 'tis not improbable, but that there may be found many *Mechanical inventions* to improve our other Senses, of *hearing, smelling, tasting, touching.*"

2. The hypercello was developed by Tod Machover and his team at MIT's Media Laboratory. A brief technical description is given in Tod Machover, "Hyperinstruments: A Progress Report 1987–1991," MIT Media Laboratory, January 1992. See also Thomas Levenson, "Taming the Hypercello," *The Sciences* (July/August 1994): 15–17.

3. The term is from "cybernetic organism" and applies to artificial and augmented bodies animated by human intelligence. In Arthur C. Clarke's 1956 novel *The City and the Stars,* for example, human beings convert themselves into cyborgs by transferring their minds into machines. More recently, the concept has been deployed to good effect by cultural critics; see Donna Haraway, *Simians, Cyborgs, and Women: The Reinvention of Nature* (New York: Routledge, 1991); and Mark C. Taylor, "The Betrayal of the Body: Live Not," in *Nots* (Chicago: University of Chicago Press, 1993), pp. 214–55.

4. For an introduction to the topic of the body in architectural and urban space, see Richard Sennett, *Flesh and Stone: The Body and the City in Western Civilization* (New York: W. W. Norton and Company, 1994). Here we're talking about flesh and bits.

5. The technology of bodynets was rapidly emerging by the early 1990s. Infrared wireless communication between electronic devices had, for example, become commonplace. (One inexpensive personal communicator became popular with school kids because its infrared capabilities allowed silent passing of electronic "notes" in class.) Conformable, wearable computers of various kinds were beginning to appear.

6. Industrial designer Emilio Ambasz has already speculated about "a soft portable telephone, a soft lap computer, a soft camera." See *I. D.* 39: 3 (May/June 1992): 28–29.

7. For a brief survey of electronic prostheses, implants, and related issues, see Gareth Branwyn, "The Desire to Be Wired," *Wired* 1: 4 (September/October 1993): 62–65, 113.

8. "How to Scan a Cat," *The New York Times Magazine,* Sunday, January 16, 1994, p. 11.

9. For a convenient summary of the early history of television, see Steven Lubar, *InfoCulture: The Smithsonian Book of Information Age Inventions* (Boston: Houghton Mifflin Company, 1993).

10. For a discussion of Xerox PARC research on media spaces, see Sara A. Bly, Steve R. Harrison, and Susan Irwin, "Media Spaces: Video, Audio, and Computing," *Communications of the ACM* 36: 1 (January 1993): 28–47.

11. This metaphor originated with the "Hole-in-Space" project of video artists Kit Galloway and Sherri Rabinowitz in 1980. The artists set up a two-way video connection between outdoor public pedestrian spaces in Century City, California, and Lincoln Center in New York City. Images of pedestrians were projected at approximately full scale, and transcontinental casual pedestrian encounters could take place.

12. *Duets,* produced by Phil Ramone (Capitol Records, 1993).

13. For a brief account of the process and of the technology employed, see Anthony Ramirez, "A Major Record Album: Only a Phone Call

Away," *The New York Times,* Thursday October 7, 1993, D1. See also National Public Radio, "A Review of Frank Sinatra's Latest Album 'Duets'," *Weekend Edition* transcript for Saturday, November 13, 1993, segment 18.

14. Hans Fantel, "Sinatra's 'Duets' Album: Is It a Music Recording or Technical Wizardry?," *The New York Times,* Saturday, January 1, 1994, pp. 11, 23. William Safire added, in a column entitled "Art Vs. Artifice" (*The New York Times,* Monday, January 3, 1994, A23): "The 'duets' are a series of artistic frauds. The singers never sang together, never interacted. Sinatra wheezed out his soundtrack and others — by telephone — laid down their counterfeit counterpoint."

15. Avital Ronell, *The Telephone Book: Technology, Schizophrenia, Electric Speech* (Lincoln: University of Nebraska Press, 1989), p. 301.

16. Elizabeth M. Wenzel, "Localization in Virtual Acoustic Displays," *Presence* 1: 1 (Winter 1992): 80–107.

17. Use of motion-based simulators for entertainment can be traced all the way back to early fairground carousels, with their bobbing wooden horses for small children. Modern motion-based simulators for location-based entertainment (LBE) installations typically have computer-controlled hydraulic actuators that move riders along up to three axes of translation and three of rotation. See Stephen Clarke-Willson, "The Design of Virtual Environments — Value Added Entertainment," *Computer Graphics* 28: 2 (May 1994): 102–4.

18. Y. S. Kwoh, J. Hou, E. A. Jonckheere, and S. Hayati, "A Robot with Improved Absolute Positioning Accuracy for CT Guided Stereotactic Surgery," *IEEE Transactions in Biomedical Engineering* 35 (1988): 153–60.

19. W. S. Ng, B. L. Davies, R. D. Hibberd, and A. G. Timoney, "Robotic Surgery: A First-Hand Experience in Transurethral Resection of the Prostate," *IEEE Engineering in Medicine and Biology* 12: 1 (March 1993): 120–25.

20. Charles Petit, "Robot's Operating Room Success: Sacramento Man Takes a Few Steps 2 Days After Surgery," *San Francisco Chronicle,* November 10, 1992, A4.

21. In 1993 NASA attempted to put an eight-legged, teleoperated robot called Virgil down the crater of Mount Erebus in Antarctica. Unfortunately, the mission failed due to a broken cable. In 1994 the Dante 2 robot made a more successful descent into the Mount Spurr volcano in Alaska; see Warren E. Leary, "Robot Is Nearing Goal Inside Active Volcano," *The New York Times,* Tuesday, August 2, 1994, C8.

22. For a brief survey of such applications, see David C. Churbuck, "Applied Reality," *Forbes,* September 14, 1992, pp. 486–90.

23. See "Robot Disarms Gunman," *Associated Press Online,* Sunday, September 5, 1993, for the story of how a teleoperated robot owned by a Maryland police department was successfully used to disarm a murder suspect hiding in a closet. According to the report, "Transmitting the scene by a video camera, the robot opened a closet door at the direction of a fire department employee who was at the controls from a safe distance."

24. Michael W. McGreevy, "The Presence of Field Geologists in Mars-Like Terrain," *Presence* 1: 4 (Fall 1992): 375–403.

25. This account is based on Alvin and Heidi Toffler, *War and Anti-War* (Boston: Little, Brown and Company, 1993), pp. 111–12.

26. Col. Frederick Timmerman Jr., "Future Warriors," *Military Review* (September 1987). For more discussion of the relevant technologies, see Steven M. Shaker and Alan R. Wise, *War Without Men* (Washington, DC: Pergamon-Brassey's, 1988).

27. Rodney Brooks, Anita Flynn, and Lee Tavrow, "Twilight Zones and Cornerstones: A Gnat Robot Double Feature," MIT Artificial Intelligence Laboratory, 1989.

28. Edmund L. Andrews, "A Robot Ant Can Be Tool or Tiny Spy," *The New York Times*, September 28, 1991. The construction of the silicon ant is briefly described in *BCS Tech* (May 1993): 3–4.

29. Warren Robinett, "Synthetic Experience: A Proposed Taxonomy," *Presence* 1: 2 (Spring 1992): 229–47.

30. Eric Drexler and Chris Peterson, with Gayle Pergamit, *Unbounding the Future* (New York: William Morrow, 1991).

31. The early histories of telegraphy and wireless telegraphy are usefully narrated in Lubar, *InfoCulture*.

32. Robinett, "Synthetic Experience."

33. This was in 1993. Equivalent technology was slower to appear in the US; see Mathew L. Wald, "An Oldsmobile Option for Self-Navigating Car," *The New York Times*, Wednesday January 5, 1994, D2, and Mathew L. Wald, "Navigating Your Auto by Computer," *The New York Times*, Tuesday, February 8, 1994, D5. For an introductory survey of the technology, see Robert L. French, "Cars That Know Where They're Going," *The Futurist* (May/June 1989): 29–36.

34. There is a well-developed technology of Geographic Information Systems (GIS). As geopositioning and mobile computing technologies develop, it becomes increasingly feasible to deliver the resources of a GIS system to precisely where they are needed in the field.

35. For discussion of flexible, electronic road-use pricing and related ideas, see M. Hepworth and K. Ducatel, *Transport in the Information Age: Wheels and Wires* (London: Belhaven Press, 1992). A section of Route 91 in Orange County, California, introduced automatic vehicle identification (AVI) devices, electronic sensors, and a "congestion pricing" system to mitigate traffic jam problems; see Suneel Ratan, "Traffic-Free Roads: Engineers Are Merging Computers and Concrete to Ease Driving's Biggest Pain," *Fortune*, July 13, 1992, p. 83.

36. A technical introduction to the issues involved here is provided in Pravin Varaiya, "Smart Cars on Smart Roads: Problems of Control," *IEEE Transactions on Automatic Control* 38: 2 (February 1993): 195–207.

4 RECOMBINANT ARCHITECTURE

1. For elaboration of this line of argument in a more recent context, see Langdon Winner, *The Whale and the Reactor: A Search for Limits in an Age of High Technology* (Chicago: University of Chicago Press, 1986).

2. William M. Bulkeley, "Libraries Shift from Books to Computers," *The Wall Street Journal*, Monday, February 8, 1993, B4.

3. This has some additional advantages. Books are brittle, but bits don't bust. Fragile old books can be preserved by storing their pages in digital format, then reprinting facsimiles where necessary on acid-free paper.

4. Steve Lohr, "Record Store of the Near Future: Computers Replace the Racks," *The New York Times*, Wednesday, May 12, 1993, pp. 1, D13; and Kevin Maney, "Revolution in Store for Record Shops," *USA Today*, Monday, May 17, 1993, B1–B2.

5. Access to the Electronic Newsstand is via Gopher or Telnet. Information is available at *info@enews.com*.

6. John Tierney, "Will They Sit by the Set, or Ride a Data Highway?," *The New York Times*, Sunday, June 20, 1993, p. 1.

7. In September 1993 Murdoch acquired Delphi Internet Services, a small online service specializing in providing access to the Internet. Plans to publish a worldwide online newspaper were announced. See Josh Hyatt, "Future Subscribers," *The Boston Globe*, Friday, September 3, 1993, pp. 71, 73.

8. Development of library and museum plans is explored in Thomas A. Markus, "Visible Knowledge," in *Buildings and Power* (London: Routledge, 1993), pp. 171–212.

9. Nikolaus Pevsner, *A History of Building Types* (Princeton: Princeton University Press, 1976), p. 106.

10. The possibility of such a library has become a topic of discussion among humanities scholars. See *Technology, Scholarship, and the Humanities: The Implications of Electronic Information* (Santa Monica: The Getty Art History Information Program, 1993), p. 23. For a general discussion of the move toward online libraries, see John Browning, "Libraries Without Walls for Books Without Pages," *Wired* 1: 1 (1993): 62–110.

11. See "US, British Libraries Need Space," *Channel DLS* 25: 8 (April 1990): 8; "Mobile Shelving Snafu: British Library Building Under Construction in London Delayed by Rusting Stacks," *ENR* 229, September 28, 1992, p. 17; and "Dispersal of Harvard Library," *San Francisco Chronicle,* March 29, 1989, A20: 1. Some soft libraries already exist. The *Thesaurus Linguae Grecae* — a very extensive corpus of ancient Greek texts — has been published on CD by Yale University Press. And a two-gigabyte British National Corpus — a national treasury of the English language — is under development. See Brian Keeney, "The Keeper of the Living Language," *Guardian* 33: 5, April 25, 1991.

12. As the British Library itself, in 1993, prepared to move to new quarters in St. Pancras, debate raged about the relative importance of traditional and electronic library services. In a letter to the *London Review of Books* (September 9, 1993, pp. 4–5) a rather Blimpish spokesperson for the "Regular Readers' Group" questioned "BL management's right to alter the British Library's traditional role as provider of public reading rooms to that of a depot supplying books in electronic form to universities and public libraries for a fee," and went on to assert, "It is a policy which completely destroys the basis for scholarly work: that is, the creation of original work from primary sources."

13. Pevsner, "Museums," in *A History of Building Types,* pp. 111–38.

14. Similar systems have been developed for the National Gallery in Washington and other museums. See Phil Patton, "The Pixels and Perils

of Getting Art Online," *The New York Times,* Sunday, August 7, 1994, section 2, pp. 1, 31.

15. Pevsner, *A History of Building Types,* p. 74.

16. A standard starting point for Frankfurt-style critiques of this development is Jürgen Habermas, *The Structural Transformation of the Public Sphere* (Cambridge, MA: MIT Press, 1989; translation of the 1962 German original). See also Noam Chomsky's powerful analysis in E. Herman and N. Chomsky, *Manufacturing Consent: The Political Economy of the Mass Media* (New York: Pantheon, 1988).

17. The idea was put forward in a presentation at the MIT Media Laboratory symposium "Digital Expression" in October 1994.

18. Thus teaching space tends to be organized much like dramatic space; the connection was made explicit by the emergence of the anatomy theater, for formal instruction of medical students, in the sixteenth century. See Markus, "Invisible Knowledge," in *Buildings and Power,* pp. 229–44.

19. This and other school plans of the Age of Reason are explored in ibid., "Formation," pp. 41–94.

20. John G. Kemeny and Thomas E. Kurtz, "Dartmouth Time Sharing," *Science* 162: 3850 (October 11, 1968): 223–28.

21. See J. M. Arfman and P. Roden, "Project Athena: Supporting Distributed Computing at MIT," *IBM Systems Journal* 31: 3 (March 1992): 550–63; and Gregory A. Jackson, "Education and Computing at MIT: A 10th Birthday Snapshot of Project Athena," *MIT Academic Computing,* Fall 1993.

22. For discussion of a pioneering exploration of teleseminar teaching, see Mark C. Taylor and Esa Saarinen, *Imagologies: Media Philosophy* (New York: Routledge, 1994).

23. D. Chandler, "Astronomy Classes Soon May Stargaze in Daylight," *The Boston Globe,* February 18, 1993.

24. See Larry Press, "Tomorrow's Campus," *Communications of the ACM* 37: 7 (July 1994): 13–17.

25. For the evolution of hospital plans, see Pevsner, "Hospitals," in *A History of Building Types,* pp. 139–58. Markus has an insightful discussion in "The Sad," in *Buildings and Power,* pp. 107–18. A comprehensive and detailed history is provided in J. D. Thompson and G. Goldin, *The Hospital: A Social and Architectural History* (New Haven: Yale University Press, 1975).

26. Both are reproduced in Pevsner, "Hospitals," in *A History of Building Types,* pp. 139–58.

27. In both cases, in fact, the task can be formulated mathematically as a quadratic assignment problem. For a classic early discussion, see B. Whitehead and M. Z. Eldars, "An Approach to the Optimum Layout of Single-Storey Buildings," *Architects' Journal,* June 17, 1964, pp. 1373–79. Early attempts to derive efficient hospital plans automatically are surveyed in William J. Mitchell, *Computer-Aided Architectural Design* (New York: Van Nostrand Reinhold, 1977).

28. John McConnell, "Medicine on the Superhighway," *The Lancet* 342, November 27, 1993, pp. 1313–14.

29. See Andrew Purvis, "Healing by Wire," *Time,* May 18, 1992, p. 68; Lou Fintor, "Telemedicine: Scanning the Future of Cancer Control," *Journal of the National Cancer Institute* 85: 3 (February 3, 1993): 183–84; Peter L. Spencer, "The Future of Telemedicine," *Consumers' Research* 76: 5 (May 1993): 38; Lisa Belkin, "New Wave in Health Care: Visits by Video," *The New York Times,* July 15, 1993, A1; C. Everett Koop, "Telemedicine Will Revolutionize Care," *USA Today,* August 23, 1993, A9; Stephanie Plasse, "The Doctor Is On-Line," *Boston Globe,* September 8, 1993, pp. 43, 45; Lance Fraser, "Remote Possibilities," *New Physician* 42: 6 (September 1993): 24; Peter Yellowlees and William T. McCoy, "Tele-

medicine: A Health Care System to Help Australians," *Medical Journal of Australia* 159: 7 (October 4, 1993): 437; Rhonda Bergman, "Letting Telemedicine Do the Walking," *Hospitals & Health Networks* 67: 20 (October 20, 1993): 46–48; Rebecca Piirto Heather, "Electronic House Calls," *American Demographics* (March 1994): 6; Gary Busack, "Rural Connections," *Health Progress* 75: 3 (April 1994): 48; and Robert S. Boyd, "Telemedicine: Two-Way Interactive Video," *Washington Post,* May 31, 1994, WH8.

30. Neil Izenberg, Director of the Nemours Center for Biomedical Communication, quoted in the transcript of "Networked Health Care Delivery: Opportunities and Challenges for the '90s," MIT Communications Forum, October 21, 1993.

31. Proceedings of the symposium "Medicine Meets Virtual Reality II: Interactive Technology & Healthcare," San Diego, California, January 27–30, 1994. Available from Allied Management Associates, *70530,1227@compuserve.com.*

32. See R. Weinstein, K. Bloom, and S. Rozek, "Telepathology: Long Distance Diagnosis," *American Journal of Clinical Pathology* 91: Supplement 1 (1989): S39–42; and R. Keil-Slawik, C. Plaisant, and B. Schneiderman, "Remote Direct Manipulation: A Case Study of a Telemedicine Work station," in H. J. Bullinger, ed., *Human Aspects in Computing: Design and Use of Interactive Systems and Information Management* (Amsterdam: Elsevier Science Publishers, 1991).

33. See B. Preising, T. C. Hsia, and B. Mittelstadt, "A Literature Review: Robots in Medicine," *IEEE Engineering in Medicine and Biology Magazine* 10 (1991): 13–22. Diana Phillips Mahoney, "Virtual Science," *Computer Graphics World* 17: 7 (July 1994): 20–26, provides a less technical survey of some pioneering attempts to develop adequately realistic surgical simulation and telesurgery systems.

34. Ian W. Hunter, Tilemachos D. Doukoglou, Paul G. Charette, Lynette A. Jones, Mark A. Sagar, Gordon Mallinson, and Peter J. Hunter, "A

Teleoperated Microsurgical Robot and Associated Virtual Environment for Eye Surgery," *Presence* 2: 4 (Fall 1993): 265–80.

35. See Proceedings of the ARPA Advanced Biomedical Technology Workshop, "Integration of Advanced Technology in the Battlefield and Operating Room," Tucson, Arizona, November 12–13, 1993, for descriptions of various physiological status monitoring systems for military personnel.

36. For useful brief histories of prison architecture, see Pevsner, "Prisons," in *A History of Building Types,* pp. 159–68; and Markus, "The Bad," in *Buildings and Power,* pp. 118–30.

37. Max Winkler, "Walking Prisons: The Developing Technology of Electronic Controls," *The Futurist* (July/August 1993): 34–36.

38. Ibid, p. 36.

39. Kirk Johnson, "One Less Thing to Believe In: High-Tech Fraud at an ATM," *The New York Times,* Thursday, May 13, 1993, pp. 1, B9. For an account of the trial of the culprits, see Steve Burkholder, "Masterminds of $107,460 ATM Caper Face Sentencing," *The Boston Globe,* Sunday, December 19, 1993, pp. 57, 59. The mastermind, Scott Pace, used the alias "Will Sutton."

40. D. G. Price and A. M. Blair, *The Changing Geography of the Service Sector* (London: Belhaven Press, 1989), p. 130.

41. Peter Passell, "Fast Money," *The New York Times,* Sunday, October 18, 1992, Section 6, p. 12. CHIPS, CHAPS, SWIFT and other elements of the large-scale, international EFT system are discussed in Allen B. Frankel and Jeffrey C. Marquardt, "International Payments and EFT Links," in Elinor Harris Solomon, *Electronic Funds Transfers and Payments: The Public Policy Issues* (Boston: Kluwer Nijhoff Publishing, 1987), pp. 111–30.

42. Pevsner, *A History of Building Types,* p. 193. Pevsner notes that the related idea of insolvency also, originally, had a very spatial and physical interpretation; when a banker turned out to be insolvent his bench was broken up — *banca rotta.*

43. For development of the idea of the virtual bank, see Robert P. Barone, "The Bank and Its Customer: Tomorrow's Virtual Reality Bank," *Vital Speeches of the Day* 59 (February 15, 1993): 282–86.

44. For discussions of these possibilities, see Burnham P. Beckwith, "Eight Forecasts for US Banking," *The Futurist* (March/April 1989): 27–33; James B. Rule, "Value Choices in Electronic Funds Transfer Policy" (Washington, DC: Office of Telecommunications Policy, undated); and David R. Warwick, "The Cash-Free Society," *The Futurist* (November/December 1992): 19–22.

45. Alan Radding, "Casino Takes a Gamble on Cashless Transactions," *Infoworld,* June 20, 1994, p. 70.

46. Thomas McCarroll, "Futures Shock: Are Trading Floors Obsolete. A New System Quickens the Race Toward a Global Electronic Market," *Time,* June 29, 1992, p. 69.

47. Reuters, "Bond System Delay Asked," *The New York Times,* Thursday, April 29, 1993, D16.

48. Peter A. Abken, "Globalization of Stock, Futures, and Options Markets," *Economic Review* (July/August 1991): 1–21.

49. John Greenwald, "The Secret Money Machine," *Time,* April 11, 1994, pp. 28–34.

50. David Tracey, "Touring Virtual Reality Arcades," *International Herald Tribune,* May 7, 1993.

51. For the shopper, the tradeoff is between the multisensory richness and possible recreational value of store shopping on the one hand and the speed

and convenience of teleshopping on the other. See F. Koppelman, I. Salomon, and K. Proussaloglou, "Teleshopping or Store Shopping? A Choice Model for Forecasting the Use of New Telecommunications-Based Services," *Environment and Planning B* 18 (1991): 473–89.

52. Pevsner, *A History of Building Types,* p. 257.

53. For an insightful discussion of the appearance of the department store and the role that it assumed in urban life, see Richard Sennett, "Public Commodities," in *The Fall of Public Man* (New York: Norton, 1992), pp. 141–49.

54. Kansas City's Country Club Plaza, built in 1922, is often cited as the prototype of the suburban shopping mall. Southdale Mall in Edina, Minnesota, built by Victor Gruen in 1956, was the first fully enclosed mall. For histories, see W. S. Kowinski, *The Malling of America* (New York: William Morrow, 1985); and B. Maitland, *Shopping Malls: Planning and Design* (Essex, UK: Construction Press, 1985).

55. Renee Covino Rouland, "Satellites Move into the Mainstream," *Discount Merchandiser* 30 (June 1990): 45–46. On VSAT technology, see Jay C. Lowndes, "Corporate Use of Transponders Could Turn Glut to Shortage," *Aviation Week & Space Technology* 126 (March 9, 1987): 122–25.

56. Stephanie Strom, "Wireless Signals Keep Retailers Humming," *The New York Times,* Wednesday, July 29, 1992, D7.

57. Francine Schwadel, "Kmart Testing 'Radar' to Track Shopper," *The Wall Street Journal,* Tuesday, September 24, 1991, B1.

58. Patrick M. Reilly, "Home Shopping: The Next Generation," *The Wall Street Journal,* Monday, March 21, 1994, R11.

59. David Bank, "After Browsing Catalogs, Dial Up Internet for Order," *San Jose Mercury News,* Wednesday, April 20, 1994, 9D.

60. In 1994 the Pizza Hut chain pioneered electronic pizza service by setting up the PizzaNet Home Page on the World Wide Web.

61. John Tierney, "Will They Sit by the Set, or Ride a Data Highway?" *The New York Times,* Sunday, June 20, 1993, p. 1.

62. One industry analyst has remarked: "Cyberspace is going to finish what Walmart started. Interactive shopping via computer networks is going to put more traditional downtowns and more mom-and-pop stores out of business." Richard Sclove, quoted by John Markoff in "Staking a Claim on the Virtual Frontier," *The New York Times,* January 2, 1994, E5.

63. This building type can be traced back, at least, to Giorgio Vasari's Uffizi in Florence, constructed in 1560–74. Downtown office buildings became increasingly popular in the nineteenth century, and — particularly in Chicago — evolved into steel-framed, elevator-serviced highrises by the end of the century. For a brief history, see Pevsner, *A History of Building Types,* pp. 213–24.

64. For an account of the evolution of this pattern, see JoAnne Yates, *Control Through Communication: The Rise of System in American Management* (Baltimore: The Johns Hopkins University Press, 1989). Early-nineteenth-century American business enterprises were usually small, family affairs in which the internal operations were controlled and coordinated through word of mouth and by letter. The railroads, the telegraph system, and later the telephone facilitated the emergence of larger and more far-flung organizations employing newer modes of internal communication and more hierarchical, systematic management techniques. New technologies for the production, reproduction, and storage of documents also played an important role.

65. Jack M. Nilles, "Traffic Reduction by Telecommuting: A Status Review and Selected Bibliography," *Transportation Research A* 22A:4 (1988): 301–17.

66. The Shenandoah Valley Telecommuting Center for federal government workers who would otherwise commute to Washington, DC is the

first installation in a federally funded pilot program. See Abby Bussel, "Telecommuting and Main Street," *Progressive Architecture* (March 1994): 55.

67. Wendy A. Spinks, "Satellite and Resort Offices in Japan," *Transportation* 18 (1991): 343–63.

68. See Kirk Johnson, "New Breed of High-Tech Nomads: Mobile Computer-Carrying Workers Transform Companies," *The New York Times,* Tuesday, February 8, 1994, B1, B5.

69. James Martin and Adrian R. Norman, *The Computerized Society: An Appraisal of the Impact of Computers on Society in the Next Fifteen Years* (Englewood Cliffs, NJ: Prentice-Hall, 1970), pp. 32, 155–56.

70. See in particular J. M. Nilles, F. R. Carlson, P. Gray, and G. J. Hannemann, *The Telecommunications-Transportation Tradeoff: Options for Tomorrow* (New York: John Wiley, 1976).

71. Robert E. Calem, "Working at Home, for Better or Worse," *The New York Times,* Sunday, April 18, 1993, Business Section, pp. 1, 6. "Telecommuters" are defined here as "employees of businesses or government agencies working part or full time at home instead of at the office." By this point, newspaper reports were increasingly suggesting that telecommuting was significantly on the rise in the United States: *The Miami Herald* (December 13, 1993, p. 24) reported that one million more people were telecommuting in 1993 than in the previous year, marking a 15 percent increase in the number of company employees who worked at home part or full-time during normal business hours; *The Wall Street Journal* (December 14, 1993, p. B1) reported that 20 to 40 percent of all employees surveyed would like to telecommute; *The Atlanta Constitution* (January 2, 1994, p. E2) reported that the trend toward electronically supported work at home accounted for 45 percent of all new jobs from 1987 to 1992; *The St. Petersburg Times* (January 3, 1994, p. 19) claimed that men's suit sales had plummeted because "dealing with people through faxes and computers" meant that "there is no need for appearance to be as large a factor."

72. Melvin M. Webber, "The Post-City Age," *Daedalus* 97 (1968): 1091–110. For similar views, see R. F. Abler, "What Makes Cities Important," *Bell Telephone Magazine* 49: 2 (1970): 10–15; and P. C. Goldmark, "Communication and Community," *Scientific American* 227 (1972): 143–50.

73. By now, there has been considerable empirical study of the tradeoffs between telecommuting and travel and of the spatial and other effects of telecommuting. See, for example, Rebecca Hamer, Eric Kroes, and Harry Van Ooststroom, "Teleworking in the Netherlands: An Evaluation of Changes in Travel Behaviour," *Transportation* 18 (1991): 365–82; Patricia L. Mokhtarian, "Telecommuting and Travel: State of the Practice, State of the Art," *Transportation* 18 (1991): 319–42; Jack M. Nilles, "Telecommuting and Urban Sprawl: Mitigator or Inciter?" *Transportation* 18 (1991): 411–32; Ram M. Pendyala, Konstadinos G. Goulias, and Ryuichi Kitamura, "Impact of Telecommuting on Spatial and Temporal Patterns of Household Travel," *Transportation* 18 (1991): 383–409; and Ilan Salomon, Helen Nancy Schneider, and Joseph Schofer, "Is Telecommuting Cheaper Than Travel? An Examination of Interaction Costs in a Business Setting," *Transportation* 18 (1991): 291–318.

74. This position is argued in Aharon Kellerman, "Telecommunications and Cities," in *Telecommunications and Geography* (London: Belhaven Press, 1993), pp. 93–115.

75. Lewis Mumford, *The City in History: Its Origins, Its Transformation* (New York: Harcourt Brace and World, 1961), p. 383.

76. By the mid-1990s, a major battle was shaping up between the computer and television industries over the characteristics of the device that would deliver bits to the home. The cable industry was pushing set-top boxes that would turn television sets into interactive devices, while personal computer companies were adding audio, video, and telecommunications capability to their products. See John Markoff, "I Wonder What's on the PC Tonight," *The New York Times,* Sunday, May 8, 1994, section 3, pp. 1, 8.

77. For discussion of this point (largely with reference to pre-computer electronic media), see Joshua Meyrowitz, *No Sense of Place: The Impact of Electronic Media on Social Behavior* (New York: Oxford University Press, 1985).

78. Alvin Toffler, "The Electronic Cottage," chapter 16 of *The Third Wave* (New York: William Morrow and Company, 1980). See also Rowan A. Wakefield, "Home Computers and Families: The Empowerment Revolution," *The Futurist* 20: 5 (September/October 1986): 18–22.

79. Kevin Robins and Mark Hepworth, "Electronic Spaces: New Technologies and the Future of Cities," *Futures* 20: 2 (April 1988): 155–76. See also Tom Forester, "The Myth of the Electronic Cottage," *Futures* 20: 3 (June 1988): 227–40.

80. See Jean-Nicolas-Louis Durand, *Précis des leçons d'architecture* (Paris: Ecole Polytechnique, 1802), for a systematic, textbook exposition of this approach.

81. For a discussion of the underlying logic of this approach, see Jenny A. Baglivo and Jack E. Graver, *Incidence and Symmetry in Design and Architecture* (Cambridge: Cambridge University Press, 1983).

82. One early example of this sort of system is Cinetropolis, developed by Iwerks Entertainment. See "Theme Parks: Feeling the Future," *The Economist* 19 (February 1994): 74–75.

5 SOFT CITIES

1. ARPANET was funded by ARPA — the Advanced Research Projects Agency of the US Federal Government — and it was intended for use by the military and by computer science researchers. For a useful summary of the early history, see Jeffrey A. Hart, Robert R. Reed, and Francois Bar, "The Building of the Internet," *Telecommunications Policy* (November 1992): 666–89.

2. The 1993, statistics are from a December 16, 1993, online posting "Revised Internet Index" by Win Treese of the DEC Cambridge Research Laboratory.

3. Accurate estimates of user numbers are hard to make, and there is some argument about these figures. See Peter H. Lewis, "Doubts Are Raised on Actual Number of Internet Users," *The New York Times,* Wednesday, August 10, 1994, 1 and D4.

4. For a history of the WELL, see Cliff Figallo, "The Well: Small Town on the Internet Highway System," September 1993, available from the author at *fig@well.sf.ca.us.*

5. Mitchell Kapor and John Perry Barlow, "Across the Electronic Frontier," Electronic Frontier Foundation, Washington, DC, July 10, 1990.

6. It seems to have first appeared on a DEC PDP-1 at MIT in 1962. It was the progenitor of increasingly fancy space shoot-'em-ups that appeared as computers became faster and graphics more sophisticated.

7. The *Picospan* software, authored by Marcus Watts to support interaction on the WELL, provided a very influential early model for this sort of virtual place.

8. Miss Manners has tackled the question of how to handle this progression. She advises: "Miss Manners would not go so far as to say that a computer bulletin board exchange constitutes a proper introduction, but she has heard worse ones. Notwithstanding, it does not confer any social obligation." *The Washington Post,* Wednesday, August 18, 1993, B5.

9. Apparently SIMNET was inspired by *Battlezone,* an Atari arcade game from the early 1980s. For discussions of SIMNET, see Warren Katz, "Military Networking Technology Applied to Location-Based, Theme Park and Home Entertainment Systems," *Computer Graphics* 28: 2 (May 1994): 110–12; Michael Harris, "Entertainment Driven Collaboration," *Computer Graphics* 28: 2 (May 1994): 93–96; and Bruce Sterling, "War Is Virtual Hell," *Wired* 1: 1 (1993): 46–99.

10. See Katz, "Military Networking," for an introduction to DIS technology.

11. The aspects of synthetic experience, and technologies currently available to provide them, are surveyed in Warren Robinett, "Synthetic Experience: A Proposed Taxonomy," *Presence* 1: 2 (Spring 1992): 229–47.

12. The phenomenon of feeling present in a virtual place has been discussed extensively in the literature of simulation and virtual environments. See, for example, Carrie Heeter, "Being There: The Subjective Experience of Presence," *Presence* 1: 2 (Spring 1992): 262–71.

13. For discussion of New York's communication advantages and their role in its growth to commercial dominance, see Eric H. Monkkonen, *America Becomes Urban: The Development of U.S. Cities and Towns 1780–1880* (Berkeley: University of California Press, 1988).

14. Though, as Miss Stein might well have judged had she encountered a newsgroup, "Remarks are not literature."

15. The City of Palo Alto was also quick to create an online information service, but took the very different approach of setting up a World Wide Web server on Internet. You can access it by Mosaic or Lynx *http://www.city.palo-alto.ca.us,* or you can get information by e-mailing to *wwwadmin@city.palo-alto.ca.us.* There is a city government phone directory, a city council agenda and meeting schedule, and so on.

16. On the development, introduction, and remarkable initial success of NCSA Mosaic, see John Markoff, "A Free and Simple Computer Link," *The New York Times,* Wednesday, December 8, 1993, D1, D5. Mosaic is essentially a point-and-click, graphic interface to the World Wide Web, an international system of database servers organized to allow remote requests for information from any computer on the Internet. The original work on World Wide Web was done by Tim Berners-Lee at CERN in Geneva in the late 1980s. Mosaic was developed at the National Center for Supercomputer Applications at the University of Illinois, Urbana-

Champaign. By early 1994, more than 50,000 copies of Mosaic were being downloaded monthly from NCSA's public server.

17. The first MUD, written at the University of Essex by Roy Trubshaw and Richard Bartle, was based on the fantasy board game Dungeons and Dragons — hence the name. There are numerous arcane variants on the generic Multi-User Something idea — TinyMUDs, MUSEs, MUSHs, MUCKs, MOOs, and so on. The differences do not matter for our purposes here. On the experience of MUD crawling, see David Bennahum, "Fly Me to the MOO," *Lingua Franca* 4: 4 (May/June 1994): 1, 22 37.

18. This is, of course, closely related to the old literary issue of establishing a voice. "Call me Ishmael" might be the opening ploy in a MUD interaction. So Wayne Booth's classic *The Rhetoric of Fiction* (Chicago: University of Chicago Press, 2nd ed., 1983) serves as a pretty good theoretical introduction to MUDding.

19. As programmers will appreciate, MUDs constitute a natural application for object-oriented programming techniques, and the developments of the MUD idea and of object-oriented programming have been intertwined.

20. Chip Morningstar and F. Randall Farmer, "The Lessons of Lucasfilm's Habitat," in Michael Benedikt, ed., *Cyberspace: First Steps* (Cambridge, MA: The MIT Press, 1991), pp. 273–302. On *Populopolis* see Howard Rheingold, "Habitat: Computer-Mediated Play," in *The Virtual Community* (Reading, MA: Addison-Wesley, 1993), pp. 188–96.

21. In Hindu mythology, an avatar is a deity descended to earth in bodily form; the word is from the Sanskrit for "descend."

22. Morningstar and Farmer, "The Lessons of Lucasfilm's Habitat," pp. 286–87.

23. Lewis Mumford, *The City in History* (New York: Harcourt Brace and World, 1961), p. 384.

24. One consequence is that you can get sued for invasion of privacy. Under American tort law, one who intentionally intrudes upon the seclusion of another is subject to liability if the intrusion would be highly offensive to a reasonable person. On the general idea of privacy rights, see Alan F. Westin, *Privacy and Freedom* (New York: Atheneum, 1967).

25. Authentication systems were not needed on the earliest computers, and they are not commonly used on personal computers today, since access to the machine can be controlled physically. But they are required on machines that have many potential users. Thus they first came into widespread use with the growing popularity of mainframe-based, multi-user, timesharing systems in the 1960s, and the idea carried over to computer networks in which a user logged into one machine can remotely access other machines.

26. You should not assume, though, that a password-protected place is necessarily private. In the widely reported case of Bourke v. the Nissan Motor Corporation in 1993, Nissan dismissed some employees after peeking into their password-protected electronic mail boxes. The employees sued for invasion of privacy and wrongful determination. But the California courts ruled against the employees' claim that the passwords created an expectation of privacy.

27. William M. Bulkeley, "Cypher Probe," *The Wall Street Journal,* Thursday, April 28, 1994, A1, A8.

28. Peter H. Lewis, "Of Privacy and Security: The Clipper Chip Debate," *The New York Times,* Sunday, April 24, 1994, F5.

29. Jerry Berman, quoted by Steven Levy, "Battle of the Clipper Chip," *The New York Times Magazine,* Sunday, June 12, 1994, pp. 44–51, 60, 70. In June 1994 the US Public Policy Committee of the Association for Computing Machinery (USACM) released an expert panel report entitled "Codes, Keys and Conflict: Issues in U.S. Crypto Policy," which took a strong stand against Clipper and urged the Clinton Administration to withdraw it.

30. Jim Kallstrom, quoted by Levy, "Battle of the Clipper Chip."

31. For a useful summary of some of the legal issues, with particular reference to electronic mail privacy and electronic monitoring of employees, see Michael Traynor, "Computer E-Mail Privacy Issues Unresolved," *The National Law Journal,* Monday, January 31, 1994, pp. 52–54.

32. For a classic discussion of the public/private dichotomy in architecture and urban design, see Serge Chermayeff and Christopher Alexander, *Community and Privacy* (New York: Doubleday, 1963).

33. Senate Bill S.2195. Inouye was serving as Chairman of the Communications Subcommittee of the Senate Commerce, Transportation and Science Committee.

34. Kevin Lynch, *A Theory of Good City Form* (Cambridge, MA: The MIT Press, 1981). See also Stephen Carr, Mark Francis, Leanne G. Rivlin, and Andrew M. Stone, "Rights in Public Space," in *Public Space* (Cambridge: Cambridge University Press, 1992), pp. 137–86.

35. The Berkeley Community Memory system, going back to the early 1970s, was a very early experiment with elements of the idea. For a survey and discussion of the first community networking efforts, see Doug Schuler, "Community Networks: Building a New Participatory Medium," *Communications of the ACM* 37: 1 (January 1994): 39–51.

36. Frank Odasz, "Big Sky Telegraph," *Whole Earth Review* (Summer 1991): 32–35.

37. Some of these issues are very basic. If you want to create a successful online public space for a multi-ethnic community, for example, you cannot rely solely on prompts and commands in English.

38. Peter H. Lewis, "Arizona Lawyers Form Company for Internet Advertising," *The New York Times,* Saturday, May 7, 1994, p. 51. On the issue of Internet advertising, see Lawrence M. Fisher, "From an Executive

at Ogilvy & Mather, Some Guidelines for Tasteful Advertising on the Internet," *The New York Times,* Wednesday, August 3, 1994, D16.

39. Peter H. Lewis, "Censors Become a Force on Cyberspace Frontier," *The New York Times,* Wednesday, June 29, 1994, pp. 1, D5.

40. There has been much controversy about Prodigy's control — and sometimes refusal to exert control — over its "public" forums; for a lively account, see Anne Wells Branscomb, "Questioning Applicable Laws: Prodigy," in *Who Owns Information? From Privacy to Public Access* (New York: Basic Books, 1994), pp. 98–103.

41. Peter H. Lewis, "Censors Become a Force on Cyberspace Frontier."

42. For discussions, see Steven Levy, *Hackers: Heroes of the Computer Revolution* (New York: Dell, 1984); and Schuler, "Community Networks: Building a New Participatory Medium."

6 Bit Biz

1. For an introduction to the bit business, see Robert Lucky, *Silicon Dreams: Information, Man, and Machine* (New York: St. Martin's Press, 1989).

2. For a discussion of difficulties in applying intellectual property law in cyberspace, see Mike Godwin, "Some 'Property' Problems in a Computer Crime Prosecution," posting on *misc.legal,comp.orf.eff.talk* of an article that first appeared in *Cardozo Law Forum* (September 1992).

3. Manuel Castells, *The Informational City: Information Technology, Economic Restructuring, and the Urban-Regional Process* (Cambridge, MA: Blackwell, 1989), p. 129.

4. For historical surveys of these places, see J. B. Jackson, "Forum Follows Function," in N. Glazer and M. Lilla, eds., *The Public Face of Architecture* (New York: Free Press, 1987), and M. Webb, *A Historical Evolution: The City Square* (New York: Whitney Library of Design, 1990).

5. Aristotle, *Politics,* VII, xii.

6. The commercial online services provide "shopping centers" that are basically conveniently organized and presented catalogues of online catalogues. On the Internet, more ad-hoc compilations like the Internet Mall have performed a similar function on a fairly small scale (for information, e-mail *taylor@netcom.com*). CommerceNet, which went online on the Internet in April 1994, is an ambitious system of World Wide Web "storefronts" accessed through Mosaic (*http://www.commerce.net*).

7. For a discussion of some of these issues, see Anne W. Branscomb, "Who Owns Your Name and Address?," in *Who Owns Information? From Privacy to Public Access* (New York: Basic Books, 1994), pp. 9–29.

8. "Prodigy Service Member Agreement," Prodigy Services Company, White Plains, 1989. For discussion, see Oscar H. Gandy, Jr., *The Panoptic Sort* (Boulder: Westview Press, 1993), p. 104.

9. List construction practices are hair-raisingly surveyed in Jeffrey Rothfeder, *Privacy for Sale: How Computerization Has Made Everyone's Life an Open Secret* (New York: Simon & Schuster, 1992).

10. Peter H. Lewis, "Attention Shoppers: Internet Is Open," *The New York Times,* Friday, August 12, 1994, D1–D2.

11. For details, see Martin E. Hellman, "The Mathematics of Public-Key Cryptography," *Scientific American* 241: 2 (August 1979): 146–147.

12. For an introduction to electronic cash schemes, see David Chaum, "Achieving Electronic Privacy," *Scientific American* (August 1992): 96–101.

13. Details on the DigiCash scheme can be obtained by sending e-mail to *info@digicash.nl*.

14. Aristotle, *Politics,* I, iv.

15. The line between agents and more traditional sorts of software tools is not easily drawn. But software is agentlike to the extent that it operates autonomously and intelligently. If it can somehow be programmed to enact your personal wishes, if it has some capacity to learn from experience, and if it can adapt to the unexpected and execute contingency plans, then you can confidently call it an agent.

16. Marvin Minsky, *The Society of Mind* (New York: Simon & Schuster, 1987).

17. Evan I. Schwartz, "Software Valets That Will Do Your Bidding in Cyberspace," *The New York Times,* Sunday, January 9, 1994, p. 11.

18. Ellen Germain, "Software's Special Agents," *New Scientist* 142: 1920 (April 9, 1994): 19–20.

19. See Pattie Maes, "Agents That Reduce Work and Information Overload," *Communications of the ACM* 37: 7 (July 1994): 31–40, 146. An early commercial example of this sort of agent was *Open Sesame!* — a Macintosh program from Charles River Analytics.

20. Some of these problems are explored in Donald A. Norman, "How Might People Interact with Agents," *Communications of the ACM* 37: 7 (July 1994): 68–71.

21. We might turn to ancient philosophy and law dealing with slaves for some guidance here, but it turns out not to be much help. Following Aristotle's view of slaves as live tools, Roman law basically denied that slaves were autonomously intelligent; they occupied some kind of limbo between human beings and animals. So, for example, a slave who killed somebody was either malfunctioning and should be destroyed or was carrying out an instruction for which the owner was responsible. The Stoics took the contrary view that slaves should be treated as autonomously intelligent beings, and Seneca famously developed the position that they were capable of virtuous action and should be held responsible for the virtue or otherwise of their acts.

22. See for instance, "Officials Fight Computerized Child Porn," *San Jose Mercury News,* Wednesday, September 1, 1993, 20A.

23. For text of the Defense Motion to Dismiss, see *Computer Underground Digest* 6: 55 (Sunday, June 19, 1994) files 1–6. On the conviction, see "Couple Guilty of Sending Pornography by Computer," *Los Angeles Times,* Friday, July 29, 1994, A10; and *Computer Underground Digest* 6: 69 (Sunday, July 31, 1994), files 1–6.

24. See Nathan Torkington, "Proposed New Zealand Legislation," *Computer Underground Digest* 6: 60 (Wednesday, July 6, 1994), file 7. The text of the bill is reproduced in *Computer Underground Digest* 6: 65 (Sunday, July 17, 1994), file 1.

25. See Peter H. Lewis, "On the Internet, Dissidents' Shots Heard 'Round the World," *The New York Times,* Sunday, June 5, 1994, E18. The Digital Freedom Network may not, in practice, be very effective, since network access currently does not reach many of the places where books are notoriously banned. It certainly would not get *The Satanic Verses* to the hinterlands of India, Pakistan, and Iran, for example. But it does establish the idea, and it suggests a very likely future condition.

26. See Ray Bradbury, *Fahrenheit 451: The Temperature at Which Books Burn* (New York: Ballantine, 1953).

27. According to a perhaps apocryphal or exaggerated story, all the broadcast networks in the old Soviet Union ran through a single switch, so that they could be shut down in an instant. True or not, this is a compelling image of totalitarian control of electronic telecommunication.

28. The contrast between centralized, potentially authoritarian, client-server architectures for computer networks and the decentralized, redundant, peer-to-peer structures and inter-networking of the Internet is explored in Roger Clarke, "Information Technology: Weapon of Authoritarianism or Tool of Democracy," *IFIP World Congress,* Hamburg, August, 31, 1994.

29. Aristotle, *Politics,* VII, v.

30. Rick E. Bruner, "Info Explosion Extends to the Former East Block," *The Boston Globe,* Monday, August 1, 1994, pp. 18–19.

31. For one view of how this might work, see D. Elgin, "Conscious Democracy Through Electronic Town Meetings," *Whole Earth Review* (Summer 1991): 28–29.

32. Recall that William Gibson's cyberspace novels postulate head implants as interface devices. When characters offend against the power structure, they risk getting their brains fried. Any kind of force-feedback device also has the potential to inflict violence.

33. This may become a standing threat and standard penalty, just as transportation to Australia became a standard penalty in the eighteenth-century British legal system.

34. An occasional criticism of online public spaces is that they represent a wimpy cop-out — a withdrawal from full-blooded engagement in real urban places with all their risks and dangers. (It's a line that seems particularly popular with New Yorkers.) I'm not so sure. There are few places nastier than the site of an all-out flame war.

35. Roger A. Clarke, "Information Technology and Dataveillance," *Communications of the ACM* 31: 5 (May 1988): 498–512.

36. On the methods of TRW and other major credit bureaus, see Rothfeder, "The Secret Sharers," in *Privacy for Sale,* pp. 31–62.

37. For development of this scenario, see Gandy, *The Panoptic Sort.*

Though there is lots of relevant and interesting material available in print, the best way to pursue further reading on the topics discussed here is to surf around in cyberspace itself. To provide a convenient starting point, an online version of this book is available on the World Wide Web. This incorporates numerous links from the text to other sites and resources, and it has online forums for further discussion of the issues. You can find it at:

http://www-mitpress.mit.edu/City_of_Bits/

In addition, the following classified list suggests some useful World Wide Web sites, Gopher sites, FTP sites, and electronic mail addresses.

Sites in cyberspace do not live forever, so this list will eventually become — like the traces of a city that is no longer inhabited — a piece of digital

S U R F   S I T E S

archaeology. Link rot will gradually set in; many of the listed addresses will cease to exist, and much of the online material will be deleted or lost. But even if you are a latecomer, and find that the zone of cyberspace mapped here is mostly a ruin when you reach it, you should still find that it gives at least a few entry points to active areas.

The information to be found out there is of very variable quality. *Caveat surfer!*

COMMERCE

Business Gateways.
http://actlab.rtf.utexas.edu/gateways/biz.html

CommerceNet Home Page.
http://www.commerce.net/

Commercial Directories on the Web.
http://works.zilker.net/com-http.html

Commercial Sites.
http://gopher.econ.lsa.umich.edu/EconInternet/Commerce.html

Experimental Stock Market Data.
http://www.ai.mit.edu/stocks.html

IMall Home Page.
http://www.imall.com/homepage.html

Interesting Business Sites on the Web.
http://www.rpi.edu/~okeefe/business.html

Internet Business Directory.
http://ibd.ar.com/

Internet Shopping Network.
http://shop.internet.net/

Open Market's Commercial Sites Index.
http://www.directory.net/

Shopping IN.
http://www.onramp.net:80/shopping_in/

Thomas Ho's Favorite Electronic Commerce WWW Resources.
http://biomed.nus.sg/people/commmenu.html

Yellow Pages.
http://www10.w3.org/hypertext/DataSources/
    bySubject/Yellow/Overview.html

Blacksburg Electronic Village Home Page.
http://crusher.bev.net/BEVhome.html

Cleveland Free-Net.
telnet://freenet-in-a.cwru.edu

Freenets and the Politics of Community in Electronic Networks.
http://www.usask.ca/library/gic/v1n1/graham/graham.html

Freenets Home Page.
http://herald.usask.ca/~scottp/free.html

MGD TapRoom.
http://www.mgdtaproom.com/

National Public Telecomputing Network: Affiliates and Organizing Committees.
http://free-net.mpls-stpaul.mn.us:8000/teleport/top.html

DIRECTORIES

EINet Galaxy.
http://galaxy.einet.net/

Internet Directory.
http://home.mcom.com/home/internet-index.html

The Whole Internet Catalog.
http://www.digital.com/gnn/wic/index.html

Yahoo-A Guide to WWW.
http://akebono.stanford.edu/yahoo/

Diversity University.
http://pass.wayne.edu/DU.html

Globewide Network Academy.
http://uu-gna.mit.edu:8001/

MIT School of Architecture and Planning Home Page.
http://alberti.mit.edu/ap/ap.html

National Distance Learning Center.
telnet://ndlc.occ.uky.edu

Virtual Online University.
http://core.symnet.net/~VOU/

ELECTRONIC CASH

CyberCash Home Page.
http://www.cybercash.com/

DigiCash Home Page.
http://www.digicash.com/index.html

First Virtual Home Page.
http://www.fv.com/

GENERAL

Alliance for Public Technology.
http://apt.org/apt.html

ECHO Home Page.
http://www.echonyc.com/

HotWired.
http://www.wired.com/

WELL Gopher Site.
gopher://gopher.well.sf.ca.us/

INTELLECTUAL PROPERTY

Electronic Frontier Foundation Intellectual Property Issues and Policy Archive.
http://www.eff.org/pub/EFF/Legal/Intellectual_property/

INTERNET

Electronic Frontier Foundation's Guide to the Internet.
http://www.eff.org/pub/Net_info/Guidebooks/
    EFF_Net_Guide/netguide.eff, ftp.eff.org/pub/Net_info/
    Guidebooks/EFF_Net_Guide/netguide.eff, or send e-mail to
    info@eff.org

Information Sources: The Internet and Computer-Mediated Communication.
http://www.rpi.edu/Internet/Guides/decemj/icmc/top.html

Internet Society Home Page.
http://info.isoc.org/home.html

The Internet Index.
http://www.openmarket.com/info/internet-index/current.html

WWW Hot Topic: Internet 25th Anniversary.
http://www.amdahl.com/internet/events/inet25.html

MUDS AND MOOS

Available Information on MUDs.
http://www.cis.upenn.edu/~lwl/mudinfo.html

MediaMOO.
telnet://mediamoo.media.mit.edu:8888

MUDlist.
http://www.cm.cf.ac.uk/User/Andrew.Wilson/MUDlist/dorans.html

NATIONAL INFORMATION INFRASTRUCTURES

Europe and the Global Information Infrastructure.
http://www.earn.net/EC/bangemann.html

IT2000-A Vision of an Intelligent Island.
http://www.glocom.ac.jp/mirror/
    www.ncb.gov.sg/it2k/it2k.html

The National Information Infrastructure: Agenda for Action.
ftp.ntia.doc.gov or gopher.nist.gov

POLITICAL ECONOMY OF CYBERSPACE

Computer Underground Digest.
Subscribe by sending e-mail to tk0jut2@mvs.cso.niu.edu with the subject
header: SUB CuD and a message that says: SUB CuD my name my.full.in-
ternet@address.

The Electronic Frontier Foundation Home Page.
http://www.eff.org/

PRIVACY

Information Security and Privacy in Networked Environments.
ftp://otabbs.ota.gov/pub/information.security

TELECOMMUNICATIONS

Telecom Information Resources on the Internet.
http://www.ipps.lsa.umich.edu:70/0/telecom-info.html

I presented a first sketch of this book at a symposium entitled *Electrotecture: Architecture and the Electronic Future,* sponsored by the Guggenheim Museum and *ANY* magazine, in New York in 1993. The results of this symposium were published in *ANY,* number 3 (November/December 1993). I am grateful to Mark C. Taylor and Cynthia C. Davidson for organizing this very successful event, and to the other participants for the stimulating discussion that they provided.

In Fall 1994, Mitch Kapor and I taught an MIT graduate seminar entitled *Digital Communities;* numerous discussions with Mitch, with our teaching assistant Anne Beamish, and with participants in the seminar generated additional ideas and insights.

ACKNOWLEDGMENTS

The final text owes much to the extensive, meticulous research efforts of Anne Beamish. Debra Edelstein provided editorial advice. Michael Baenen did some crucial fact checking. Friends, students, and colleagues too numerous to mention read versions of the manuscript as it evolved and generously gave me their comments.

The jacket illustration was produced by Suguru Ishizaki at the MIT Media Laboratory, using concepts of three-dimensional typography developed by the late Muriel Cooper. The plans in chapter 4 were all drawn by Anne Beamish. Additional illustration credits are as follows: page 2, photograph courtesy of NYNEX Corporation; page 6, drawing by P. Steiner, © 1993 The New Yorker Magazine, Inc., All Rights Reserved; page 26 top, Leonardo da Vinci, "The Proportions of Man," The Bettmann Archive; page 26 bottom, still from the film *Lawnmower Man;* page 46 top, Eugène-Emmanuel

Viollet-le-Duc, "The First Hut," from *The Habitations of Man in All Ages,* translated by Benjamin Bucknall (London: Sampson Low, 1876); page 46 bottom, *Punch,* December 19, 1878 (Punch's Almanack for 1879); page 106 top, detail from Giambattista Nolli, *Nuova Pianta di Roma* (Rome, 1748); page 106 bottom, e●World screen shot courtesy of Apple Computer, Inc.; page 132, Krzysztof Wodiczko, photographs courtesy of the artist; page 162, photograph © Serge Lafontaine and Tilemachos Doukoglou, courtesy Ian Hunter.

Access controls, 9, 21–24, 121–124, 149–151, 159

Access privileges, 17–18, 117, 124–128, 155

Action at a distance, 38–40

Actuators, 40

Addresses, 8, 10–11, 68

Advertising, 62, 129

Aga Khan, 68

Agents, 13–15, 143–146, 178n13, 206n15

Agora, 7–8, 167, 176n2

Alexandria, 56

Aliases, 7, 11, 12, 14, 15

Architecture, physical, 43, 44, 46

Architecture parlante, 48

Aristotle, 8, 111, 139, 143–144, 151, 152, 206n21

ARPANET, 68, 107–109, 110, 150, 198n1

Artificial intelligence, 144–146

Asynchronous communication, 15–17

Athena. *See* Massachusetts Institute of Technology

Australia, 68, 163–165, 166

Authentication, 122, 142

Altair, 109

Alte Pinakothek, Munich, 57–59

Altes Museum, Berlin, 57, 59

Amateur Action Bulletin Board, 147–148

American Graffiti, 62

America Online, 108, 120, 130, 155

Amsterdam Stock Exchange, 84

Anonymous remailers, 10

Ant robots, 39

Apple Computer, Inc., 106, 109, 178n15

Architectural types, 47, 103

Automatic teller machines (ATMs), 78 79, 81, 111 112, 158

Automobile sales, 91

Baird, John Logie, 32

Bandwidth, 17–18, 19, 20, 180n28

Banishment, 154–156

Bank of China, Hong Kong, 93, 94

Bank of England, London, 80, 81

Banks, 78–82, 93, 94, 111–112, 141–143